SPECTRUM SECRETS

SPECTRUM SECRETS

The Untold Stories of Parents With
Autistic Children

Dr. Sharline Mashack

Copyright 2019 by Sharline Mashack, DNP, PMHNP-BC

All rights reserved. This book may not be reproduced, copied and/or distributed in any manner whatsoever without written permission except by a reviewer who may cite brief quotations to be included in a review. Thank you for purchasing this book.

For more information, please visit www.drmashack.com.

Book Cover Design by Chi Byrd
Edited by Lee Caleca
Book design by Maureen Cutajar (gopublished.com)

ISBN: 978-1-7343003-0-7 (print)
ISBN: 978-1-7343003-1-4 (ebook)

Disclaimer

The purpose of this book is to provide enlightening and helpful information on the subjects addressed in this publication. It is not intended as a substitute for the medical or health advice of physicians, or any other professional services. The author and publisher advise readers to consult with their medical, health, other competent professional prior to implementing any of the book's suggestions or drawing inferences from this publication.

Although every attempt to ensure the information in the book was accurate, the author and publisher do not assume and specifically disclaim all responsibility for any liability to any party for any loss, risk, damage or disruption which is incurred as a result from indirect or direct use and application of any material in this publication.

This book contains recreated conversations, events, and settings from my memories. In order to maintain their anonymity, I have intentionally changed the names of individuals, places, and any recognizable details, and in some scenarios, conversations from a few individuals have been attributed to one. Modifications were carefully considered to maintain the true essence of each story while achieving the main objective: to reveal open secrets (emotions) many of us experience but never freely discuss. Therefore, if you envision yourself within these stories, it is purely coincidental.

Acknowledgements

Your experiences in life are created through the quality of your thoughts. Sometimes, the Lord allows us to go through pain to prepare us for our purpose. I'm eternally thankful to God for His wisdom, favor, and mercy which allows me to serve others for His glory.

Sharing my story was harder than I thought and more rewarding than I could have ever imagined. The inspiration for this book would not have been made possible without my genuinely caring son, Gregory. He has taught me how to love beyond words. He is the epitome of unconditional love and my reason why. I see your true colors, and that's why I love you. Buddy, I will always have your back!

I'm forever grateful to my amazing husband, Tray, who encouraged me to follow my dreams and has made countless sacrifices to ensure I accomplished my goals. Your devotion to our family has allowed me to live my best life without regrets. You have taught me about perseverance, communication, time-management, and selfless love. Not only my best friend, you have been my shoulder to cry on, my rock to stand on, and the love of my life.

My world would not be complete without my loving son, Tristin. You have given me so much hope and motivation to continue being the best version of myself. You have taught me how to live life to the fullest and not to stress over the little things. I am so honored God chose me to be your mom and friend. You are destined for greatness and we will be there every step of the way. You are an exceptional son and caring brother and God will continue to bless you for being your brother's keeper.

To my family. Mommy, thank you for all your sacrifices, love, and devotion throughout the years. You have taught me how to serve others without expectation and I'm so honored to be Daphne's daughter. You are my everything! My loyal brothers and sisters, thank you guys for your unwavering love, sincere advice, and support from day one. My dear aunts, uncles, and cousins - you all make my heart smile! You guys give me the inspiration to continue believing in myself and I'm grateful to call you family. My loving In-laws: I am so grateful for God-fearing parents who continuously pray and shower our family with unconditional love and guidance. You guys always remind me that God answers prayer. My thoughtful extended family - I am truly blessed to have you all in my life to love and support me in ways I didn't know I needed. Family forever and always…and no matter what!

To my sister-friends. Our sense of humor is a like a rare gem. You guys continue to keep me laughing, even on days when I forget how much I have to smile for. We share so many memories and secrets, I couldn't get rid of you guys if I wanted to. Your non-disclosure agreements are in the mail. Friends are the family you choose—I love each and every one of you.

To my editorial/support team. You guys have always inspired me to share my story with the world. Thank you for helping me turn my ideas into a reality. Special thanks to Jake, Jessica, Brent, Jackie, Kim, my college professors, Greenlight family, Jacksonville School of Autism family and the countless caregivers who have supported my family throughout the years. A very special thanks and appreciation to Lee Caleca, my highly proficient editor who has a keen eye for excellence and attention to detail.

Contents

INTRODUCTION: The Devastating Diagnosis 1
PART ONE: What is Autism Spectrum Disorder (ASD)?. 9

SECRETS REVEALED

    Shock/Disbelief. 15
    Anger. 16
    Guilt 18
    Fear/Panic 20
    Embarrassment 22
    Frustration. 25
    Shame. 26
    Resentment 33
    Sadness/Grief 35
    Worry/Anxiety 39
    Desperation 41
    Jealousy. 42
    Loneliness 44
    Betrayal. 46
    Exhaustion. 48
    Excitement. 51

PART TWO: Where Does Your Child Fit In? 53
The Three Types of Autism Spectrum Disorders

WHAT THEY DIDN'T EXPECT

Poor/No Eye Contact. 56
Non-Responsiveness 58
No Communication 61
Non-Verbal Communication 64
Social Anxiety. 66
Repetitive or Odd Behaviors 68
Poor Motor Skills 69
Tuning Out. 71
Wandering 73
Temper Tantrums and Sensory Meltdowns. 78
Dealing with tantrums and meltdowns 80
No Pretend Play. 83
Attachment to Hard Inanimate Objects. 86

Author's Note 89
Where Are They Now? 93
About the Author. 109
References. 111
Resources 117

"Owning our story can be hard but not nearly as difficult as spending our lives running from it. Embracing our vulnerabilities is risky but not nearly as dangerous as giving up on love and belonging and joy—the experiences that make us the most vulnerable. Only when we are brave enough to explore the darkness will we discover the infinite power of our light."

– Brene Brown

Introduction

The Devastating Diagnosis

"Autism doesn't come with a manual; it comes with a parent who never gives up"

It only took four words to destroy my world forever! Four words that pierced my heart with a jagged knife, leaving broken pieces to an unknown puzzle.

"Your son has autism"

It seemed as though something had changed about him overnight, and Wes, my happy energetic toddler, was never the same. All of a sudden, he lost his smile, his voice, his personality. Just like that, everything just stopped!

His cheerful giggle was replaced by a high-pitched, monotonous squeal. "EEEeeeeEEEeeeeeEEEeeeee", Wes repeatedly screeched while assembling his hot wheels in a single-file line.

He became fascinated with objects that moved in a circular fashion, from trains and helicopters to ceiling fans and toilets.

Life as I knew it would never be the same! A thousand questions ran across my mind, as my eyes filled with disbelief. I was devastated!

My son has WHAT?! WAIT...what is Autism? How do you know for sure? How could this be? Like Rain Man? Is there a blood test? Did I eat something wrong? Is it genetic? Can I get a second opinion? Did I skip my prenatal vitamins? Did I eat too much fish? Did I sleep on my stomach? Did I hurt my baby? How could this happen to me? I saw something about vaccines, could that be it? I did everything right!! He never missed an appointment, he got all his shots on time. How can this be? Why me? Why him? Why us?

Fighting back tears, I sat and stared, ultimately sinking into a dark place—somewhere I'd never been. It was worse than any nightmare I could have imagined.

While staring at the blank walls inside this cold office, my bare shoulders no longer needed a sweater to stop the shivering, my body no longer felt anything at all. I was frozen, unable to move, think, or speak. My world was shattered into a million pieces. I was empty from the inside-out!
　"Hello, ma'am… are you ok," the doctor asked.
　My lips were quivering as I replied.
　"Yeah." Of course I was lying, but that was the only answer I could give without breaking down in front of my child.
　"So how do we fix this? Is there a medication for it?" I asked.
　"I'm sorry, ma'am, there's no cause or cure that we know of," the doctor explained. He handed me a brochure on autism and gave me a recommendation for speech and occupational therapy.
　The brochure read:

Autism is a developmental disorder characterized by marked deficits in communication and social interaction, preoccupation with fantasy, language impairment, and abnormal behavior, such as repetitive acts and excessive attachment to certain objects. One in 250 children are affected by Autism Disorder…

At that very moment, all hope and optimism were gone! I don't even know 250 people. I didn't know who to call, where to go, what to think! All I knew was that the little boy I imagined had vanished before my eyes. No college graduation, no weddings, no job, no grandchildren.

And no answers, no cause, and no cure!

"No, No, No, No! Not My Baby!"

All of sudden, my heart overflowed with its own blood, suffocating every breath I tried to take. The beautiful Florida sun no longer shined across my face. The darkness of my eyelids blocked the penetrating sunshine, while every teardrop burned the windows of my soul. My husband tried to console me, but his words fell on deaf ears. His usual comforting words provided no solace or satisfaction. I could only hear the doctor's voice in my head.

"Your son has A-U-T-I-S-M."

Those words played like a broken record to a song you hate but know all the words to. I lost my appetite, I lost my confidence, I lost my motivation, and I lost the life I envisioned for my son.

Wes was born a "typical" baby with no health problems. He had reached all the milestones, some even earlier than expected. Then around age two, I noticed he started regressing and losing language. And by the time he was four, he had stopped talking and went into another world. My fight with autism was over before it started. I lost everything I dreamed of about having a baby, and autism won the war.

When I decided to write this book, I knew I would need to find a way to explain the pain I felt. I hate reliving that moment but it's the only way to make people understand the devastation parents go through—but no one talks about. There's a lot of shame that seems to be thrown at us just for being honest, even though most of the research suggests it is an environmental trigger and not something the mother did. However, the exact cause remains unknown.

Similar to dementia, your loved one changes right before your eyes. It's very complicated because you love your child, but hate the disability. You recognize your child's potential, but can't see their future.

You constantly mourn the loss of the child you envisioned.

Most parents give birth to seemingly healthy babies, who unexpectedly develop autism. This life-changing discovery can be disappointing, leaving parents feeling helpless.

As a board-certified mental health professional, I've encountered many parents who suffer from depression, stress, and anxiety due to the challenges surrounding autism. It is a chronic condition which causes a lifetime of sorrow for some individuals. The mental turmoil can have a negative impact on a person's physical, emotional, and spiritual well-being.

If you're reading this book, you're likely a parent, caretaker, or family member of an autistic child. Autism conferences, support groups, parenting magazines, and blogs may provide some insight into your concerns, but this book will give you an understanding into what others like yourself are feeling—what they're going through. You will know you're not alone, and this may be some small comfort. Your emotions will be validated knowing that what you're feeling is real. Keep in mind it's okay to be that, to feel that, whatever it is for you. You don't need to be ashamed or hide your feelings.

The insight you gain into your emotions as a parent or caregiver will be nourishing and validating for you. It will help you get through the days with more hope and will allow you to see your autistic child in a different way. No, he or she may never be the child you envisioned for both your child and yourself, but you will learn that there is a way to understand and connect that you hadn't expected.

And this will give you the courage to move in the right direction—a direction where there is growth.

This beautiful child of yours is an exotic creation, and however little you understand him or her, you will recognize growth in yourself and in your child regarding their nature and your own, for you will discover things about yourself you couldn't possibly have accessed otherwise.

And it's in those moments, when you see a spark of recognition—some small connection—that your heart will soar. You may still feel overshadowed by sadness, but if you can love with your mind as well as your heart, you will find some solace in small growth.

You may feel isolated and abandoned by your loved ones. Most people are unsure of what support is desired and will withdraw themselves emotionally, leaving a void in communication. Unintentionally, they are leaving a void in loving you and your family because you're left to suffer alone, perhaps in silence. Your loved ones may be unaware of your terror, your deep grief, and your need to have someone you can talk to.

If you're married, your spouse will have his/her own grief and will process everything surrounding this differently than you. But know that he/she is suffering as well. If you have other children, they may not understand any of this and will need special conversations with you to help them understand. Keep it simple.

Something that may surprise you, however, is your autistic child's ability to "connect", even nonverbally, with a sibling, another child with a soft personality, or a quiet adult. They can sense certain vibrations coming from certain people. In the reverse, sensing anxiety, meanness, or unsettled personalities is often what makes them anxious around others.

I was surrounded by supportive family and friends who offered heartfelt advice like "God only gives these kids to special people" or "God doesn't put more on you than you can bear". However, this well-intended advice never made me feel "more special" than anyone else. I spent years suffering in silence, feeling helpless because I couldn't undo what happened to my child; I failed to protect him. Although it is the natural order of life, I feared dying (even in old age); the thought of leaving my child in this cruel world was unbearable. As a young girl, I have always been passionate about helping others but I couldn't help my own child. I never intended to work in mental health, but as a special needs parent, I wanted to "fix" my child and that's what sparked my interest in psychiatry.

Eventually, I learned my inner pain had a purpose, and then my life CHANGED! I knew my child needed me to stay healthy, physically and emotionally, as long as possible. Maintaining a positive attitude and reframing my feelings allowed me to accomplish my goals and live a more fulfilled life. My positive energy even influenced my child's behavior, which fostered his independence. I found my joy by bringing joy to others. My goal is to positively transform the lives of families who are affected by autism so they have better emotional well-being to deal with worry, loneliness, guilt and unconscious self-destruction.

"What happens to my child when I DIE?"

This lingering worry is common among special needs parents. The time of one's death is uncontrollable. However, many parents fail to take action towards improving their physical/emotional health—the very thing they can CONTROL! Emotional stress leads to inflammatory responses which is the catalyst for most diseases and disorders. It is critical for parents to take charge of their emotional/physical wellbeing to improve the quality of their lives and remain healthy advocates for their loved one with a disability.

In this book, I will give you insight into the unpredictable emotions you'll be feeling as you and your child go through life. I will provide useful information to increase your awareness about the history, symptoms, and facts regarding autism. The book not only provides real-life stories, but offers informative facts and practical solutions to improve your child's behavior, reframe your reactions, and positively transform your perspective. In addition, this book provides references of positive affirmations and inspiration quotes.

Each of the stories presented comes from someone who is going through what you're going through. Each of these men and women are at different stages of grief, enlightenment, and understanding, and each has experienced an array of mixed feelings associated with chronic sorrow. These feelings are common, and you will experience many of them at different times. These emotional responses are subjective and can be triggered by any number of things.

You will cry and maybe even smile as you see yourself and your child in them. Allow these experiences to nurture your personal growth and development as we unravel these *Spectrum Secrets* together.

Part One

What is Autism Spectrum Disorder (ASD)?

"I am different. Not less." (Dr. Temple Grandin)

First, let me make it clear that ASD does not discriminate. It occurs across all ethnic, racial, and economic groups and usually appears within the first two years of life. Worldwide, it affects boys nearly five times as much as girls. You didn't do anything wrong. In fact, ASD has become so prevalent that the American Academy of Pediatrics now recommends that all children be screened for autism.

The word *autism* was first used in 1911 by German psychiatrist Eugen Bleuler. At that time, it was used to describe a subset of severe schizophrenic patients who were especially withdrawn and self-absorbed (Evans, 2013), but scientists now believe there is no link between the conditions.

According to Bleuler, autistic thinking was characterized by "infantile wishes to avoid unsatisfying realities and replace them with fantasies and hallucinations". *Autism* defined the subject's symbolic 'inner life' and was not readily accessible to observers". (Bleuler, 1911 as cited in Moskowitz, 2011)

By 1943, Leo Kanner, M.D. used it to describe children who were highly intelligent but displayed "a powerful desire for aloneness" and "an obsessive insistence on persistent sameness."

In the 1960s, the idea of "infantile thought" was challenged and autism was completely reframed. Child psychologists used the word to describe the *exact opposite* of what it had meant up until that time. Instead of excessive hallucinations and fantasy in infants, it now referred to a complete lack of an unconscious symbolic life. For example, Michael Rutter, a leading child-psychiatric researcher from the UK's Maudsley Hospital who conducted the first-ever genetic study of autism, claimed in 1972 that "the autistic child has a deficiency of fantasy rather than an excess". (Rutter, 1972) The meaning of the word autism was then radically reformulated from a description of someone who fantasized excessively to one who did not fantasize at all.

- By 1987, UCLA psychologist Ivar Lovaas, Ph.D had published the first study showing how intensive behavior therapy can help children with autism, giving new hope to parents.
- In 2000, vaccine manufacturers remove thimerosal, a mercury-based preservative, from all routinely given childhood vaccines due to public fears about its role in autism.
- In 2013, all subcategories were placed under one umbrella: autism spectrum disorder, defined by impaired social communication and/or interaction and restricted and/or repetitive behaviors.

Simply speaking, ASD is essentially described as a disorder that affects communication, social skills and behavior. As the parent or caretaker of an autistic child, you know this is about as basic as it can get, and it goes far beyond social avoidance and repetitive behaviors. There will be difficulty, to say the least, with communication, if there's any at all. Interaction with other people can be extremely limited. These reasons alone are enough to cause anxiety, but there are other symptoms. ("Autism", 2019)

Here are some signs that may indicate your baby should have a developmental evaluation, according to the Centers for Disease Control and Prevention (Lord, 2006) He or she:

BY 3 MONTHS
- doesn't respond to loud noises
- doesn't follow moving objects with her eyes

- doesn't grasp and hold objects
- doesn't smile at people
- doesn't babble
- doesn't pay attention to new faces

BY 7 MONTHS
- doesn't turn her head to locate where sounds are coming from
- shows no affection for you
- doesn't laugh or make squealing sounds
- doesn't reach for objects
- doesn't smile on her own
- doesn't try to attract attention through actions
- doesn't have any interest in games such as peekaboo

BY 12 MONTHS
- doesn't crawl
- doesn't say single words
- doesn't use gestures such as waving or shaking her head
- doesn't point to objects or pictures
- can't stand when supported

BY 24 MONTHS
- can't walk
- doesn't speak more than 15 words
- doesn't use two-word sentences
- doesn't seem to know the function of common household objects, such as a telephone, fork, and spoon
- doesn't imitate your actions or words
- can't push a wheeled toy
- doesn't follow simple instructions

AT ANY AGE
- loss of previously acquired speech, babbling or social skills
- avoidance of eye contact

- persistent preference for solitude
- difficulty understanding other people's feelings
- delayed language development
- persistent repetition of words or phrases (echolalia)
- resistance to minor changes in routine or surroundings
- restricted interests
- repetitive behaviors such as flapping, rocking, spinning, etc.
- unusual and intense reactions to sounds, smells, tastes, textures, lights and/or colors
Not all children will show all behaviors.

SOCIAL COMMUNICATION / INTERACTION BEHAVIORS MAY INCLUDE:
- making little or inconsistent eye contact
- tending not to look at or listen to people
- rarely sharing enjoyment of objects or activities by pointing or showing things to others
- failing to or being slow to respond to someone calling their name or to other verbal attempts to gain attention
- having difficulties with the back and forth of conversation
- often talking at length about a favorite subject without noticing that others are not interested or without giving others a chance to respond
- having facial expressions, movements, and gestures that do not match what is being said
- having an unusual tone of voice that may sound sing-song or flat and robot-like
- having trouble understanding another person's point of view or being unable to predict or understand other people's actions

RESTRICTIVE / REPETITIVE BEHAVIORS MAY INCLUDE:
- repeating certain behaviors or having unusual behaviors; repeating words or phrases, a behavior called echolalia
- having a lasting intense interest in certain topics, such as numbers, details, or facts

- having overly focused interests, such as with moving objects or parts of objects
- getting upset by slight changes in a routine
- being more or less sensitive than other people to sensory input, such as light, noise, clothing, or temperature

People with ASD may also experience sleep problems and irritability. Although people with ASD experience many challenges, they may also have many strengths, including:

- being able to learn things in detail and remember information for long periods of time
- being strong visual and auditory learners
- excelling in math, science, music, or art
- lack of awareness of personal identity allows for intense focus

The bottom line is this: science and awareness change with every passing day, and new developments are made. We know a lot more today than we did 100 years ago.

For you, right now, however, here's what you should know about what to expect. And remember, everyone goes through this, so you shouldn't feel isolated or embarrassed in any way about what you're feeling.

What They Didn't Expect

"I'm not in this world to live up to your expectations and you're not in this world to live up to mine." (Bruce Lee)

In the 1960s, Swiss-American psychiatrist Elizabeth Kűbler-Ross defined various stages of grief, with the original model inspired by her work with terminally ill patients. I believe receiving a diagnosis of autism can have the same effect on parents. You'll go through denial, anger, bargaining, depression, and finally acceptance.

There will always be exceptions to the rule, but in general, these are the common emotions and/or concerns expressed by parents and caregivers of children with autism. You may not experience all of them, and there is no particular timeline for going through them. Some may come earlier and some later. Some will repeat in your life and many can be set off by certain triggers.

This list is intended to provide insight and awareness to families so they know they are not alone in their feelings and frustration.

1. Shock/disbelief
2. Anger
3. Guilt
4. Fear/panic
5. Embarrassment
6. Frustration
7. Shame
8. Resentment
9. Sadness/grief
10. Worry/anxiety
11. Desperation
12. Jealousy
13. Loneliness
14. Exhaustion
15. Excitement

Despite these mixed emotions, you will experience many beautiful and unforgettable moments with your child. You have the privilege of hope if you choose it, and then growth will come for you and your family.

SECRETS REVEALED

These Are Their Stories

"Display a wound, the proud scars of combat." (Leonard Cohen, *The Favorite Game*)

These are the confessions of parents with autistic children, and there are thousands of stories that remain unspoken. These stories highlight the emotional triggers and feelings associated with the event.

Shock/Disbelief

"There is no point in using the word 'impossible' to describe something that has clearly happened." (Douglas Adams)

Sandy is a nurse and married with two children. She's always been a healthy eater and an energetic person—an over-achiever.

Sitting in the doctor's office after taking her two-year-old in for odd unresponsive behavior, she was given the diagnosis of autism.

"At first I was in **shock**. I literally stood there looking at the pediatrician. I just stood there, shaking my head and frowning. I was in **denial**, in **disbelief**. This couldn't be right. He was wrong. Surely there was some mistake.

"I took James home and went about my regular routine as though nothing had changed. When my husband came home, I told him I was going to change pediatricians. I told him why.

"The next day I did exactly that. In fact, I changed pediatricians four times until the reality finally hit me. My son was autistic. It was then that I began to **rage**. I didn't cry for a long time. Instead, I would be doing something routine like folding laundry and would throw the basket against the wall and pound my fists on the dryer, yelling at the same time.

"This went on for weeks until I finally exhausted myself. And then the tears came."

Transformative Takeaway

The trigger for Sandy was the initial diagnosis of autism. Receiving a diagnosis of autism may be challenging and difficult to process. You will require a new mindset to manage your frustrations and make appropriate decisions for your child. In some cases, a diagnosis of autism causes conflict between parents, with one parent in denial and the other parent accepting the diagnosis. If you suspect your child has ASD, you should consult your child's pediatrician or find a specialist who is qualified to recognize ASD. The longer you avoid getting a diagnosis, or an evaluation, the more you'll delay the possibility of educational and behavioral therapies that can help your child. Early intervention may reduce the severity of communication and behavior problems associated with ASD.

Anger

> "Letting go gives us freedom, and freedom is the only condition for happiness. If, in our heart, we still cling to anger, we cannot be free." (Thich Nhat Hanh, *The Heart of the Buddha's Teaching: Transforming Suffering into Peace, Joy, and Liberation*)

Jennifer is a widow and mother of four. She's an overweight loner who experiences chronic fatigue, nonetheless she is highly devoted to her children and her dog.

"The thing I remember most is how angry I was at the time. I had Marcus registered into a great daycare facility, one that was difficult to get into. It wasn't cheap, but it had specialized programs, a proven curriculum with school-readiness tools, and took infants to school age children, so I'd be able to keep him there until he started school. They had an opening and he was accepted, with full payment of course.

"On the second day, the teacher called me at home and told me I needed to pick Marcus up because he was being extremely fussy and could not be calmed down. I thought maybe he was sick or just getting used to the other kids.

"When I got there, there didn't seem to be any problem, but I was told that since it was already three o'clock, I should take him anyway. I had to leave work to pick him up and now could not go back.

"The following day, he was fine. No phone calls. But on the fourth day, I was called again to pick him up. 'What is it this time? What is he doing that's so awful?' I was told he was taking toys from another child and not sharing. I just wanted to scream at her that he was only two, but I bit the bullet and left work again to go get him.

"By the way, I was also told that on the third reprimand, he would be removed from the daycare permanently. I'm usually very easy-going but it was difficult for me to keep my mouth shut. I did, however, because I'd paid a lot of money for this and didn't want to make any waves.

"When I got home with Marcus, he seemed to be fine. He played with his toys quietly and I began to think about his behavior. At that point, he hadn't been diagnosed with autism. I remembered how he, several times, had insisted on not sharing his toys with his sister, who was just four. I simply chalked it up to age or sibling rivalry. I really didn't think much of it, but he was scheduled for a regular checkup that week and I thought I'd ask the doctor about whether or not this was normal. I thought it was.

"When I got the diagnosis of autism, it was clear as a bell that all the odd little behaviors that I thought were normal were symptoms of autism. I did take him back to daycare the next day and there was no trouble, but that only lasted a day. On the following day, he was expelled. I was asked not to return him to the facility because he was disruptive.

"The **anger** welled up in me like nothing I'd ever felt before. What was the big deal with him not wanting to share toys? I became ugly. I said my piece and stormed out of the facility with my son in my arms, wrapping him up as though this would protect him from all the evil naysayers who were making him out to be some kind of misfit.

"I was angry for months. I went around scowling and retreated into myself. I became bitter. It was me and my children against the world now. Looking back, I can see I was being irrational, but at the time, it seemed as though the whole world was against me—no, not me, my son. Was there no place for him in society? This was my predominant thought and it kept me isolated for a long time. I feel as though I've wasted years of my life in anger."

Transformative Takeaway

For Jennifer, the whole idea that her child should be made an outcast was infuriating, and it turned her inside out. She needed help and guidance—resources to let her know that there was support out there for her son and her situation. Learn more about effective stress management techniques and coping skills using www.drmashack.com.

Guilt

> "But what if I should discover that the most impudent of all the offenders, the very enemy himself [is] within me, and that I myself stand in need of the alms of my own kindness—that I myself am the enemy who must be loved?" (C.G. Jung, Memories, Dreams, Reflections)

Denise is a people-pleaser. She's a homemaker who's friendly to just about everyone, but she tends to be sedentary, staying home all day, eating junk food, and watching TV in her down time. Her son Evan had already been diagnosed with ASD and was entering first grade.

"It was during the IEP meeting that I began thinking about how I might have played a big part in this whole thing. I'm not much for trying to eat healthy, I pretty much just always grab what's convenient. By the time I get through doing everything I need to do each day, all I feel like doing is laying on the couch and watching TV, usually with a bag of chips and a can of Coke.

"But sitting there, my mind started to wander to all the times I'd drunk coffee while I was pregnant, two or three cups a day loaded with sugar, sodas and chips for supper many nights, skipping breakfast most days, and eating a fast-food burger or PB&J for lunch.

"Could food really have that much of an affect? Suddenly, the counselor was calling my name. I hadn't been paying attention. 'Evan has certain limitations and we need to provide him with miniscule goals. In this way we can track his progress and abilities growth,' he was saying.

"'Mmm.' I just nodded my head and had this sort of blank wide-eyed stare on my face. My mind was elsewhere. How many cans of Coke did it take to cause this? I knew I could have done better. I knew while I was indulging myself that I should have been eating healthy, but I was lazy.

"The **guilt** I felt nearly consumed me. I stopped eating junk and began obsessing over eating healthy. Everything suffered—my housework, my wardrobe, my grooming, my garden, my hair—everything. I spent every waking moment on the computer looking for healthy recipes or in the kitchen preparing great food. I'd actually lost a few pounds but I looked a wreck.

"One day, a friend of mine stopped over and was shocked at my appearance. 'What the hell happened to you?' 'What do you mean?' 'You're a mess!'"

"It was like some sort of intervention, and it was then that I realized I was trying desperately to assuage the guilt I felt over my son's autism. Now, I've changed course just a bit and I devote more time to finding foods and therapies that can help him rather than allowing myself to be consumed by guilt."

Evan had not gone to daycare or preschool. He'd managed to make it through kindergarten because the school system in her county was equipped to handle challenged children like Evan, but first grade was going to be a greater challenge.

Transformative Takeaway

When Denise realized that her child might not advance along with the rest of his peers, she became overwhelmed with feelings of guilt and began obsessing about eating right. She would cry silently in her bed at night, feeling very much alone, and thinking that she could have avoided this for her son. In the end, however, she found a healthy balance for both of them.

Guilt is a common emotion expressed by many parents who are desperate to find a reason for their child's diagnosis. However, left untreated, guilt can lead to negative changes in one's personality. It is important for parents to understand they are not to blame for their child's diagnosis. Remember, you did nothing wrong, it is NOT YOUR FAULT. Discover practical methods to alleviate self-destructive feelings which hinder your emotional well-being at www.drmashack.com.

Fear/Panic

> "Can a man still be brave if he's afraid? That is the only time a man can be brave." (George R.R. Martin, Game of Thrones)

Morgan is a bit introverted, but he's a terrific dad and devoted husband. He's neat and organized, and naturally overprotective of his six-year-old autistic son, Matt.

"I couldn't believe what was happening. There I was, sitting at a red light on Imperial Boulevard with Matt in the back seat, and suddenly, out of nowhere, he jumps out of the car and starts running down the street, back the other way. The Boulevard is one of the busiest streets in town—two lanes in each direction with a grass median in the middle and stores on both sides.

"I was in the left-hand lane and couldn't pull over. I panicked. I wanted to turn off my engine and abandon the Range Rover to run after Matt. But in that split second that I'd hesitated, he was nowhere in sight. The little bugger just took off. I had the doors locked and he must have unlocked his side.

"I've been through a war, but I don't think I've ever been as afraid as I was in that moment. This was a kid who was smart—very smart. Who knew what he would get into or where he would go? His curiosity might have led him anywhere—or worse, with any one.

"The light had turned green and I was still looking in the rear-view mirror trying to spot him. I was planning to get over to the right and turn into one of the parking lots, but people behind me started honking horns. Didn't anyone notice a kid jumping out of a Range Rover and taking off down the street?

"I probably should have turned off the engine, turned on the flashers, locked the vehicle and run after him right then. But several minutes had now already passed and I was still trying to get into the right lane. My heart was racing and I was sweating. I was in full **panic** mode. **Fear** had taken over me in the same way soldiers fear the unknown on the battlefield. But this was my son. Where had he disappeared to so quickly?

"Within about four to five minutes, there was a cop on the scene. More time was wasted with his questioning me about what was going on, but I guess it needed to be done. At that point, he radioed for assistance and stopped traffic so I could move the Rover off the road. Then we sprang into action.

"In the meantime, I was unsure if I should call my wife. An hour had now passed and we were only supposed to be going to buy new trainers for Matt. It was Saturday and the mall would have been crowded, but an hour would have been about all the time it should have taken to get to the mall, get the shoes, and return home. Then my cell rang. It was Julia, my wife.

"'Where are you guys?' I think she could hear the panic and fear in my voice, but I was still hesitant to tell her what was going on. Then she heard the police radio. 'What was that? Is everything okay?' I had to tell her what happened, very briefly. 'Please don't panic. We'll find him. He's a smart kid.'" But I wanted to cry.

"It took myself and probably eight or ten police to finally find him roaming around a candy store we'd passed on the way to the mall. It was about half mile back from where he'd jumped out of the truck.

"I was almost unfit to drive home. I was trembling, my hands were shaking, and I felt like I might pass out. I called Julia and she and my dad came together to get us so one of them could drive the Rover back home. It's a day I'll never forget. And I'll also never forget to turn the child safety locks on. I don't ever want to feel that fear again."

Transformative Takeaway

What makes a child do something like this? Most children are naturally curious, but autistic children can be obsessive. When they want something, they have no filters about getting it. They place laser focus on the object of desire and, in their view, it's just a straight line from here to there. Matt, even at six, was unable to grasp the concept of danger (jumping out of a vehicle in traffic). He only knew the candy was there and he was going to get it.

Embarrassment

> *"Life should come with a trapdoor. Just a little exit hatch you could disappear through when you're utterly and completely mortified. But life does not come with a trapdoor."* (Michele Jaffe)

Tina is a married, middle-aged mother of ten-year-old Emma. She's a wealthy, easy-going, animal-loving extrovert.

"I hate these things. Family reunions. I love my family, but sometimes I'd just rather keep my distance. They always want to be in my business. I know they mean well—maybe. But sometimes they can be judgmental.

"So everything was going fine. We got out of the house with no problems getting Em to finish dressing herself. I like to give her something to eat before we go to this type of function. That way she's not "in the food". We were on time for a change.

"There were other kids there. Cousins and a few children of other guests, and a lot of them were about the same age as Emma. My husband's brother has a big property, so the kids were running around, playing in the area that was set up for them. All of a sudden some of the boys came into the crowd of adults, laughing and screaming.

"My heart immediately jumped into my throat. I reached for my cigarettes and lit one up. I had a sinking feeling it had to do with Em. Sure enough, she had taken her top off and was walking around like a proud peacock showing off her non-existent breasts.

"I could see the disgust and judgement on the faces of some of the women, my sister-in-law included. They were huddled together, whispering and looking my way. When I saw Diana, my husband's sister, coming in my direction, I stubbed out my cigarette and braced myself. It was embarrassing to say the least, and I knew she was going to add insult to injury. There was going to be a scene.

"'Why do you let her do things like this?' Those were the first words out of her mouth. She was leaning in to me in a threatening manner. What the hell? 'You have no idea how embarrassing this is to me. I have important guests here. A lot of them are Jack's associates.'

"Embarrassing to her? I was shaking my head in disbelief. Not only was I **embarrassed** by what Emma was doing, but now I was being made out to be a negligent parent, doubly embarrassed by her criticism. And believe me, it wasn't going unnoticed by the rest of the family. They were all looking in our direction. Admittedly, Diana has always been a bit of a self-righteous jerk, but this was not the time to 'school' her.

"I wanted to just leave, but I knew I had to stay in "the scene of the crime" to begin to change Em's unacceptable behavior. I calmly walked over to Emma and took her hand. I asked her where her shirt was and she pointed over to the swings. We walked there together and I asked her to put her skirt back on, telling her that when she is around other people, it's important to keep all her clothes on.

"The kid had no problem with this. Too bad the adults weren't as sensible. When she was fully dressed, we left.

"I haven't spoken to my sister-in-law since. The men talk, but I'm not going to let that woman dictate my happiness. Emma is *my* daughter and if Diana isn't intelligent enough to understand the complex issues I go through *every single day*, then I don't need her in my life, and certainly not in my daughter's life."

You're going to meet many people with domineering personalities: the loud, the obnoxious, those that noisily stake their claims in your territory and everywhere else they set foot on.

> *"Predators want to dominate because that makes them feel strong and important. The truth is that predators have no strength and no courage. I have lost many a friend over the fact that when they attempt to rip me, they can't." (C. JoyBell C)*

TRANSFORMATIVE TAKEAWAY

Behavioral therapy functions on the idea that all behaviors are learned, but in Emma's case, she didn't understand where the line was between behaviors that are acceptable for a three-year-old and a ten-year-old. This has more to do with her underdeveloped sense of societal norms rather than her will to be defiant in any way.

Tina did the right thing. She stayed at "the scene of the crime" as she put it so Emma might understand within the setting of the occurrence. This also demonstrated to Tina's family that she was a good parent with skills beyond what they might have understood.

Frustration

> *"Frustration is a feeling of being upset and irritated, and eventually helpless to do anything to get away from it; the feeling that no matter how hard you're trying, you're not getting anywhere, and you don't even know the reason this is happening."* (Payal Kanjwani)

Jeff is in a situation that might be unique to many men, but is on the rise. He's a single father of two boys, twelve-year-old Josh and seven-year-old Jacob who has only recently been diagnosed with having a pervasive developmental disorder. He doesn't quite fit into the classic autism spectrum and has significant challenges in social development.

"We've been dealing with this kid for a long time. There was so much strife going on in this house it just got to the point where my wife left me. She wanted a divorce. I got custody of the boys because I'm a stay-at-home dad. I've got my own problems. My hip is fused to my spine making it impossible for me to hold down a regular job. I can't stand or sit for long periods of time and my mobility is limited. I'm an overweight mess. And on top of that, I asked my mom to move in with me because I don't want to put her in a nursing home. She just can't take care of herself anymore. What am I supposed to do?

"So last weekend, my friend Marc invited us over to his house for a cookout. I thought it would be great for the boys to do something other than stay in the house playing video games. I feel bad for Josh because he's the older one and I rely on him a lot to help me with Jake and Mom, but today he was going to just have fun.

"Well at one point, we looked around and there was no Jake. Everyone started looking for him and Marc finally found him in the bathroom, toilet stuffed with toilet paper, water running all over the floor, and there's Jake sitting in the water having a good old time.

"I was so **frustrated** at that point that I just grabbed him by the arm and shook him. I know this was the wrong thing to do, but I was overwhelmed. It just seemed like there was never going to be a moment's peace where we could just go out and have fun without wondering where the next horror story was going to happen.

"Marc calmed me down and said not to worry about it. It was easily fixable and no real damage was done, but I don't know if I can take any more. And what about Josh? That poor kid; I feel like I'm spending never-ending amounts of time on Jacob and less and less time with Josh."

Transformative Takeaway

For parents like Jeff who are really unable to cope at times, there are respite services available. A respite provider is an individual who is paid by the state to provide "respite" services for families, basically giving parents and siblings a break from the autistic child. The respite provider takes care of the child for a few hours during the week, providing temporary relief for the caregiver; the provider comes to your home and you are free to do what you like, gain some perspective, and get some much-needed time away from every-day cares.

Shame

> "Shame, blame, and the withholding of affection damage the roots from which love grows. Love can only survive these injuries if they are acknowledged and healed." (Brené Brown, *Daring Greatly: How the Courage to Be Vulnerable Transforms the Way We Live, Love, Parent, and Lead*)

John had seen two tours of duty during the Iraq War; four years each, from 2003 to 2011. He's a Command Sergeant Major, selected by the Department of the Army; the epitome of success in his chosen field, handsome and a bit cocky. These men are chosen because of their energy and enthusiasm even in the worst of times. In his job, he's expected to be calm, settled, and unequivocally accurate.

His wife Barbara had been pregnant with their second son when he entered the service, and John Jr., their first son, was five. He had been a handful then, but nothing had prepared John for the son he no longer knew.

"We were living off base and JJ had just started middle school. I wanted to do things with him—get to know him better. I was sure his behavior was the result of my not being around enough, that a man's influence—my influence—would straighten him out. If I could handle a bunch of grunts, surely I could train one thirteen-year-old boy.

"So we went to a soccer practice at school. JJ wasn't part of the team, but I wanted to get him interested in some sport, something he could channel all that energy into. He was fine in the car, doing his usual thing; counting cars—counting red cars. When we got to the field, he started becoming a bit antsy, like he didn't want to get out of the car, and did a little foot stomping and head banging.

"I've seen soldiers get like this. Not exactly like this, but I've seen them become very anxious, nervous, jittery—like they were afraid but didn't dare express that. They were supposed to be brave men. Surely this kid of mine wasn't going through that. Could it be?

"I managed to soft-talk him the same way I did with my men. I wasn't a drill sergeant—the guy who intimidates soldiers into submission and duty; I was the guy who used intelligent motivation to get men to do what they were trained to do. JJ bought it. But I wasn't sure what was actually going on in his mind. He seemed to withdraw into himself.

"I was sitting on the bottom bleacher, wearing my fatigues. I pretty much always wear them. JJ was off to my right on the grass, just standing there at first, watching the team. The next thing I knew, he started twirling in circles, looking up at the sky, and droning; some screeching sound, kind of like a baby who can't talk yet.

"I was having a tough time ignoring him. I felt as though everyone was watching him. Here's this thirteen-year-old kid acting like he was three. A couple of boys passed by him and sniggered. I was embarrassed, but more to the point, I was **ashamed**—ashamed of my own son.

"I've seen men die in combat, but never felt shame over my role in getting them there, and here I was, ashamed over something that was completely out of my control. Still, I felt some courage to make this right—to make this child of a very different war not die like the others; I didn't want my son to die, to be non-existent, not in his mind or in mine."

Transformative Takeaway

John's shame stemmed from his years in the military, where everything was orderly and responsiveness was immediate. He never had to second-guess his decisions regarding the behavior of those under his command. Now, he felt his son's behavior reflected his own character and shortcomings.

Fortunately for both John and JJ, John was patient and disciplined, so when he decided to take action, he sought a plan and was 100 percent committed to finding solutions, regardless of the measures he would need to take to reach his goal. Military life was filled with ranking officers, drills, and learning skill sets, so John did what he knew best.

Improving your child's behavior

Ironically, much of the training John learned in the U.S. Army is very similar to the behavioral methods and tools given to parents in this situation. Here are some of the ways John was able to use his military experience to help.

1. Timing is everything

In a combat situation, timing and communication are critical. In fact, soldiers rely on everything being timed to perfection. John reasoned that if he could create some regular precision in JJ's routine, his son would begin to see this as part of a cycle, just like counting red cars.

Most kids don't like to leave something while they're playing. They become so focused on what they're doing, it's difficult to break them away. For autistic children, trying to drag them away from whatever they're focused on can result in tantrums or extreme meltdowns.

In military training, a whistle is used to start and stop certain training maneuvers. John used a whistle—the same kind referees use—to signal JJ one minute before it was time to stop whatever he was doing. He used one minute because this was a short enough time frame to stay fresh in the mind, but long enough for the brain to begin to 'unwind' from its intense focus.

"Sixty seconds can go by pretty fast. Men working their way through an obstacle course become more invigorated; adrenaline and the thought that they want to finish pumps them up and heightens their awareness. It worked for JJ.

"It didn't work all the time at first. At the start of a game, going to the park, reading, or whatever he was going to do, I told him he would hear a loud whistle "later", and that would mean it's almost time to go or stop what he was doing. I didn't place a time limit on him, but I knew when the whistle would blow. I blew the whistle for him so he would know what to listen for.

"The first few times, he looked up from what he was doing and I told him he had one minute left to continue in this activity. When I blew the whistle the second time, I said 'time to stop' and he showed just a little resistance. In his mind, I believe he simply needed some form of boundary, some structure. I wasn't actually forcing him to do anything. He was sort of allowed to process the fact that it was time to stop. After about two weeks, I began to see real results."

You may not need to carry a whistle around with you. Most cell phones have timers that will work just as well for you. Just make it loud enough for your child to hear. The actual sound is what breaks their focus.

2. SETTING GOALS

It's difficult for most children to set any kind of long-term goal, but they do understand that if they do 'this' they will then be able to do 'that'. It's the traditional "first/then" model.

"This was really a no-brainer for me. During basic [referring to Army Basic Training or Boot Camp], you learn to accomplish tasks—things like marching, grooming standards, proper dress, and so on. Recruits know that if they don't do 'this', they won't get to do 'that'. Of course, in the army, I'm dealing with adults who can reason sufficiently. So I wondered how I could go about instilling this ethic in JJ.

"We do a lot of training videos in MOS [referring to training for a military occupational specialty] along with hands-on training. But the videos are a classic teaching tool. I needed to find a way to transition this type of training into a model JJ could relate to.

"He's actually creative, and on Saturday I watched him as he carefully cut out pictures and used glue sticks to paste them onto a piece of construction paper. It was like he was making what I would call a story board or maybe a vision board. That's when an idea hit me.

"JJ loves cars. I guess a lot of guys like to collect them, from models to the real thing, but he only has a few Matchbox cars. I think my wife felt like too many toys would be overwhelming, and more for him (or her) to pick up when he was done playing with them. So I got a catalog of model cars.

"We went through it together and used removable Post-It tabs to mark the pages of cars he liked. The he went back and carefully cut them out. My wife had an unused scrapbook and he was to paste the pictures into the scrapbook. Next to each picture, he was to write what he needed to do to get that Matchbox car. Things like finish his meals every day for a week, or make sure he put his clothes into the hamper in his room. It was sort of a reward system, but he knew that if he did 'this' he would get 'that.'"

People have different learning styles, no matter what the age or affliction, and a surprising number of autistic children think in visual images—pictures. For JJ, seeing the cars he wanted was inspiration enough to get him to do the necessary things like finishing meals, taking showers, and getting properly dressed.

3. Positive reinforcement

"You're not going to get men to do what's necessary on the battlefield by constantly screaming at them. People need encouragement and validation. So it didn't make any kind of sense to yell at JJ for doing the things he did, whether I liked it or not. He could be trained, and I was determined to use everything I learned in the military to get him there. Don't get me wrong; I would never use the exact language on a child that I use on grown men and women, but there were certain psychological tools that would work on him, and one of them was positive reinforcement.

"It was simply a matter of praising him for doing something well, like creating his scrapbook or putting his clothes away. This seemed to have more of an effect when it came to things he struggled with, like following directions. But I never talk to him in 'baby talk' and I try not to use the words 'no' and 'don't' a lot.

"To reinforce good behavior even further, and to measure his progress, I used stickers. Car stickers, of course. Every day he finished his meals, he got a sticker. He knew that when he got seven stickers, he would get one of the Matchbox cars in his scrapbook. Another thing we did was take pictures of the cars when he got them so he could glue the photograph next to the catalog cutting. This was a very tangible reward for him."

Using positive reinforcement along with focusing on what you want your child to do rather than what he's doing wrong is a great way to change behavior. For example, JJ always wants to walk in the street where the cars are. Telling him the street is for cars only and the sidewalk is for people makes sense to him. So "Don't walk in the street" becomes "Walk in the grass or on the sidewalk". "Don't glue pictures on the walls" becomes "Only glue pictures into your scrapbook".

4. Averting a crisis

"JJ rarely has meltdowns, but I've seen a lot of soldiers in this type of crisis. The fact that he was a teen and experiencing hormonal changes didn't help. So the first time it happened, I was already well-equipped, but I imagine most parents wouldn't be.

"I was in the midst of a crisis situation. I knew I needed to remain calm. It's very common for a behavioral crisis or emotional meltdown to become contagious. Soldiers work in synergy, and when emotions are running high, we all feel it. I didn't want this situation to trigger my own emotions.

"At this point, safety is always the number one priority. JJ's thirteen, but at five-feet nine-inches and a hundred and forty pounds, I knew he could do some damage if he wanted to. I knew he wasn't going to respond to reason because people in this state can't reason. The key was to talk quietly and not too much. So far, he didn't seem like he was going to hurt himself. All he was doing was tearing up his room, throwing stuff around and mumbling loudly. I don't know if this will work for everyone, but I told him I was going to the Corvette Museum and asked him if he wanted to come. This immediately got his attention and he calmed down enough for me to ask him why he was throwing his stuff around. He told me he couldn't find one of his cars.

"We searched around and finally found it, so crisis averted. We then proceeded to have a very pleasant day."

In a crisis situation or meltdown, the first priority is safety, as John suggested. Create a safe zone in your home where there is little that can be knocked down, thrown, or bumped into. This should be a place where you can keep an eye on your child and still remain out of harm's way. In an extreme emergency, you may need to call 911.

Teens are always a work-in-progress, so teaching coping skills can serve them well through their teen years and into adulthood. Once the crisis is over, discuss what set him or her off to begin with and make a plan that will make it better next time.

Parents of teens often feel isolated, but autistic teens present a challenge that can be exhausting for the entire family. Try to recognize patterns that lead to blow-ups—triggers or hot buttons that escalate tension. For parents of teenage girls, that time of the month will be another trigger. Diet is extremely important. Talk to your pediatrician about foods that are calming or have your child checked for food allergies, which are often responsible for mood swings, sleep disturbances, and outbursts.

Resentment

> *"There sprang up between the husband and wife… a silent warfare, hidden from outsiders and tempered by decorum."*
> *(Leo Tolstoy)*

Shannon is a lawyer turned homemaker who is married to a successful businessman. She has three boys and is a woman with a lot of energy who doesn't have time for housekeeping. In fact, she loathes it and would rather hire help than do it herself. She also finds herself resenting her husband who gets to go off on business trips while she's stuck home with three children.

"I love my boys and my husband, but I gave up a lucrative career to stay home and take care of my family. Now I'm starting to feel resentful of the fact that Mike gets to go away on business trips while I'm stuck here doing all this mundane stuff.

"I really don't like feeling **resentful** of Mike. He's the one who supports the family, but he's become kind of disconnected with us. I know he's focused on providing a better quality of life here, I mean, after all, taking care of a special-needs child can get a bit costly. But I really feel like he should be putting in his fair share.

"When he gets home, he seems to not want to take part in anything that has to do with any of us. He needs to chip in, be part of this family. If he's not on the phone with a client, he's in his office working on something. He shouldn't be bringing his work home with him. We need him, too. The boys need him. And what's worse, I'm starting to resent the kids, too, and it's not their fault.

"I feel like I'm just getting more and more bitter about having given up my career, and now the entire load of raising kids and running a household is on me. I haven't had a pedicure in almost a year, my hair needs cutting, and the only time I get to socialize with my friends—not that I have that many left—is if I invite them over for coffee or something. They don't even want to come over anymore.

"I know I shouldn't be blaming him. We've been married for fifteen years. I should be able to talk to him, but he never seems to have time to sit down with me. Maybe I'm just not communicating what I'm feeling. I used to be an attorney, for God's sake, I should be able to at least talk to my husband."

TRANSFORMATIVE TAKEAWAY

Resentment is very powerful and has the ability to corrode a relationship. Shannon was a giver, but she began to feel like she was the only one giving in this family dynamic. She felt deprived of her former life and therefore resented her husband because she felt he had the freedom to come and go as he pleased. What she didn't recognize was that Mike was doing the best he could and didn't realize how she was feeling. She never talked about it. Resentment is not a shortcut to resolution. Had she communicated her feelings, they might have worked things out sooner.

Shannon's resentment of her husband's apparent freedom from the obligations of putting time in with the family made her bitter and negative. What she didn't notice was that this was one of the reasons her friends were beginning to drop away.

Resentment can build slowly over time until you don't recognize who you are any more. You hide your feelings in a forest of other negative thoughts. You hurt and feel as though you haven't been treated fairly. You feel angry yet you still try to remain peaceful. You need to release your resentment.

- Take a good look at why you feel the way you do, then write it down. Keep a journal. This is extremely helpful for recognizing whether or not your feelings are founded in what's really happening or if they've simply built up in your mind to the point where they're now out of proportion to the situation.
- If you have to actually make an appointment with your spouse, do it. Make sure he or she knows there is a serious matter you need to discuss and it's to be done at a time when there will be no interruptions.
- Get a respite worker to come to your home so you can go out for a few hours and talk quietly.
- Holding your feelings in has only made your resentment grow, so try to remain respectful when expressing your feelings. You may find the situation looks completely different from your spouse's point of view.
- Create a strategy through open honest communication.
- Schedule time for doing things with friends or taking some 'me' time.

"Once we are honest about our feelings, we can invite ourselves to consider alternative modes of viewing our pain and can see that releasing our grip on anger and resentment can actually be an act of self-compassion." (Sharon Salzberg, Real Love: The Art of Mindful Connection)

Sadness/Grief

"The worst type of crying is the kind that happens when your soul weeps, and no matter what you do there's no way to comfort it. A section withers and becomes a scar on the part of your

soul that survived. For people like me, our souls contain more scar tissue than life." (Katie McGarry, *Pushing the Limits*)

Denise is single mother. She's a bank teller by day, wannabe rock star by night who sports tattoos and pink hair. When she decided to have a birthday party for her seven-year-old daughter, Melanie, she was excited about putting up glittery decorations, making cupcakes with pink icing, and getting Melanie a beautiful princess party dress. She'd invited all her family and their kids, neighbors, and schoolmates, but when the day and time of the party arrived, only three people showed up: her parents and one of the neighbor kids.

"I was deeply **sad** beyond all understanding. I kept making excuses for why no one came, but my parents knew the real reason. Melanie was a nightmare. She's my child and I love her as much as any mother could, but I knew that for others, it was almost impossible to be around her for very long. Other parents thought she was a bad influence on their kids.

"I guess it's my fault. She's already seven and should be behaving better than she does. We've been at this for four years already. I have a pretty tough skin, but getting through that day was harder than anything I've been through so far. I needed all my emotional strength just to keep from breaking down in front of everyone.

"We sang Happy Birthday, ate a few cupcakes, opened the two presents, and then everyone left. Melanie didn't even seem to notice one way or another.

I'd read Dostoevsky's *Crime and Punishment* in college, and at that moment, when I waved goodbye to my parents as they drove off, a line from that book came to mind: '*The darker the night, the brighter the stars, the deeper the grief, the closer to God.*'"

"Melanie was sitting on the couch and playing with a doll, singing to it. She sounded mournful. I'm not a musician, but I know when I hear a sad song. Tears sprang to my eyes like a flood running down my well-made-up face. There were no sobs, just water, and I don't think I've ever felt a deeper loneliness than I did right then.

"When I felt the little hand take mine in hers, I turned to look down at Melanie's face. She had pink icing smeared onto her blonde hair and a pink cupcake in her other hand, which she lifted up to me, like some sort of comforting peace offering. In that moment, in that brief connection, I knew she understood. And I knew that I loved her more than anything in the world, others be damned.

"They say laughter is the best medicine. I realized she had put the pink icing in her hair to emulate my pink hair and I started laughing. It wasn't a chuckle or a giggle, but the belly laugh of someone who is truly in a moment of joy. It was a bold hearty laugh, and to my surprise Melanie started laughing too. I suspect she was only laughing because I was laughing, but I knew we would be okay, even if being okay meant being okay alone together. This was my kid."

Transformative Takeaway

Pervading sadness is something that is extremely common among parents of autistic children. It's an emotion that saps all the energy out of a person, penetrates every part of their existence, and is present is everything they do. It's an underlying theme that can be a constant barrier to moving forward with the child's development.

Steps for building emotional toughness

"Strength does not come from physical capacity. It comes from an indomitable will." (Mahatma Gandhi)

1. Stop feeling sorry for yourself or your child. It is okay to cry at times but don't stay in that state of sadness for too long. Find the strength to focus on things that make you feel grateful. You will soon realize happiness doesn't mean things are perfect. Instead, you can still feel joy beyond the imperfections.

For Denise, she recognized that finding humor in the situation released a lot of the anguish of grief and brought her closer to her daughter in ways she couldn't have imagined before.

2. Be open to change. You may be fearful of changing the routine you've grown accustomed to, but the more you resist finding ways to help yourself and your child, the longer you'll spend not gaining any ground. You may be blocking your own growth and keeping your child from opportunities that can help him or her develop. If you've been praying for something to change, you must take the steps to make change happen.

In Denise's case, she decided that she would have another birthday party for Melanie. Only this time, they would both dress up in princess dresses and go to the park, where they would pretend to talk to the birds. It was a silly game, but the change—breaking from the conventional expectations of what a birthday party should be—made a huge difference in Denise's outlook.

3. Know what you can and cannot control. Release those people and events in your life that are causing you emotional pain. You're only responsible for yourself and your child. The only thing you can control is your reaction to situations as they occur.

There was no way Denise could have predicted the outcome of the birthday party at her house, but she was able to make the decision to have another party where she was not susceptible to the whims or decisions of others.

4. You'll never be able to please everyone. It doesn't matter what you do, how well-educated, experienced, or wealthy you are, there will always be someone who is not happy with the way you're running your life or how you're parenting your child. All that really matters is that you make the right decisions for you and your child. Don't allow the judgements of others make you into a people-pleaser.

Denise took that advice to heart. She tried to make a party that would be a great time for everyone, but in the end, she learned that Melanie wasn't interested in big shows. She was, however, interested in her mother's pink hair and made the association with the pink icing and the cupcakes. They were able to please each other, the only two people who mattered.

5. Nothing happens overnight. It took you nine months to have your child and you've had to put up with the crying and screaming and frustration that goes along with that. Think of toughening up your emotions in the same way. It's going to take some time. The idea is not to become hardened, but to be aware of your emotions and control them without suppressing them. Watch out for what sets you off, what makes you sad, and learn to express your sadness in other ways. You can take up painting or writing in a journal. Sometimes just getting it out of your system this way provides relief. Be kind to yourself and seek professional counseling if you think you cannot do this on your own.

When almost no one showed up for Melanie's birthday party, Denise felt a deep grief, as though she and her daughter were insignificant and unloved. But she recognized that she still had the power to act and she pushed through. She managed to turn her negatives into a positive. She regarded herself as a corporation of one and built her team with her daughter.

Worry/Anxiety

> *"How would your life be different if you stopped worrying about things you can't control and start focusing on the things you can? Let today be the day you free yourself from fruitless worry and take effective action on things you can change."* (Steve Maraboli, Life, the Truth, and Being Free)

Angela is an IT specialist who works for a large corporate retailer. Her husband Don also works in a corporate environment, and together they manage to have an active social life. But they have an adult child with autism who is unable to take care of herself, and they worry constantly about her safety and mortality. Who's going to take care of their daughter when they're gone?

"I never stop worrying about her. We both do. She's actually able to do a lot for herself, but there's a big problem when it comes to bathing. She likes to eat soap.

"We're both in our late forties. Marilyn is almost thirty. She's otherwise a verbal, functional college grad. She drives well and has managed to hold a full-time job as a delivery driver.

"One day, about a year ago, she started vomiting and couldn't stop. We took her to the doctor who ran some tests, and could find nothing wrong. She was fine for a few days after that, then it happened again and this time she was vomiting and experiencing severe diarrhea. She was having abdominal cramps and had a fever. This time we went to the emergency room. They did more tests and found surfactants in her stool. She'd been eating bars of soap and the liquid hand soap we keep on the bathroom vanity.

"We never would have known what it was but the ER doctor told us these surfactants are found in cleaning products like soap. So far, we've been unable to break her of the habit and I have to be in the bathroom with her while she's showering.

"I'm glad she drives for a living. If she worked anywhere that had a bathroom, she'd be in there drinking the liquid soap from the hand-washing units."

Transformative Takeaway

Many adults with autism are not extremely difficult to care for. They can follow directions and are usually honest and straightforward. Everything is literal, so they're able to follow instructions to the letter. But they often have object fixation, which was the case for Angela's daughter, Marilyn. For some reason, she became fixated on eating soap.

Marilyn is among the ten percent of high-functioning autistic adults who are able to hold down a full-time job, but having your adult autistic child out of the house all day and around other people can cause stress, anxiety, and worry.

At some point, you will need to transition your child from a pediatrician to a specialized trained psychologist, psychiatric/mental health nurse practitioner, or psychiatrist. Behavioral therapy can prepare him or her with social and communication skills, but can also deal with potentially dangerous fixations like Marilyn's.

Desperation

> *"This is one more piece of advice I have for you: don't get impatient. Even if things are so tangled up you can't do anything, don't get desperate or blow a fuse and start yanking on one particular thread before it's ready to come undone. You have to realize it's going to be a long process and that you'll work on things slowly, one at a time." (Haruki Murakami, Norwegian Wood)*

Casey is the daughter of wealthy parents. She's the mother of two children on the Spectrum. Bradley is seven and has been diagnosed with Asperger's. He's manageable, but still needs attention. Brittany is five and suffers from severe bouts of crying, biting, tantrums, as well as occasional violent hitting and scratching of her mother and brother.

"I'm committed to going to support meetings, but I have to bring Brittany with me. A lot of the parents do, and that can make the meetings a bit crazy to say the least. We never know whose kid is going to act up or what the surprise is going to be.

"Well, this time it was me. I don't even know what set her off. I think it was one of the other kids playing with a toy she wanted. I always bring her favorite toy or game but something caught her eye and she wanted the other kid's toy. And I couldn't calm her down. It became a frenzy on my part to get her to settle, not only for my sanity, but I felt like the others were getting annoyed. I don't know why I should feel that way. After all, we all had the same problem.

"But I became **desperate**; I wasn't able to think clearly. Maybe because everyone was watching and waiting for me to deal with this. She hadn't been sleeping well to begin with, and now she was in a full-blown tantrum, scratching and biting me."

TRANSFORMATIVE TAKEAWAY

Brittany has severe behavioral issues that went with her developmental disability (DD). Her mother, Casey, lacked the sense of coherence necessary to deal with that. She could not seem to adjust to the constant stress, and although she was attending meetings with like individuals, she needed more social support.

Mothers and fathers of children with DD consistently report high levels of parenting stress, weaker SOC, and poorer health than parents of children without DD, with 84% of mothers' and 67% of fathers' scores falling within the clinical range (Oelofsen, 2006).

Casey believed her locus of control was external—that it came from the behavior or actions of others, or from luck or fate, not from something she was doing or not doing. She hadn't taken it upon herself to learn any of the skills and tools that would help her and Brittany. Because she grew up in a wealthy family, she was rarely held accountable for her actions, and this informed her parenting style.

Jealousy

> "Jealousy is the most fruitful mother of tragedies. But reprehensible though it is, jealousy is almost rather to be pitied than blamed—its first victims are those who harbor the feeling." (Arthur Lynch, Moods of Life)

Stacy is a single woman who does not consider herself very attractive. She's loves to bake and likes being a homemaker, but lives on disability income, a fixed amount that does not take her very far. She's the mother of twenty-two-year-old Justin, whose cousin is about to graduate college.

"It was really hard for me to sit there and watch my sister's boy graduate. He's the same age as Justin and I feel like my son should also be up there getting his college diploma. He's not a stupid person. I know I sound **jealous**, and it's not my nephew's fault by any means. I'm not blaming anyone, it's just that... well you know... I want so much for my son and it feels like all those dreams are shattered. They're not going to happen for him.

"So then we had to go to the graduation party. We didn't "have to go", but it was the right thing to do. I didn't want to give in to my feelings and take it out on my nephew. He deserves what he deserves. He worked for it. I just can't help wishing the same kinds of happiness for Justin. It's hard. He's a young man now and what's his future going to be?

"I guess I just need to press pause. Right now, I'm just confused; I feel like we're moving in circles. I am grateful for one thing though—although Justin is unable to grasp certain adult concepts, his motor skills are great. He likes to help me bake, so we have that in common. At least I have that. It brings us both some joy.

"As I was standing there, at the graduation party, filled with guilt over my jealousy, something amazing happened. Justin and I had baked the graduation cake and Anne, my sister, called Justin up to the table just before she was about to cut the cake. She announced to everyone that he had baked the cake and he got a huge round of applause. I just started crying. I guess there is a God. And he's in my kitchen."

Transformative Takeaway
Stacy began to cultivate new ideas about her baking. She focused on things Justin could do. He was good with all the labor work, so she laid out the ingredients, he did the labor, she decorated the

intricate stuff, and surprisingly, he was able to come up with interesting ideas. They began to bake in volume and she was able to generate some additional income

Stacy was doing more of what nurtured her and her son and less of what was causing her stress about his future. She found a way to forget about what he couldn't do by focusing on his strengths.

Loneliness

> *"The most terrible poverty is loneliness, and the feeling of being unloved."* (Mother Teresa)

Tonya is a kind and gentle extrovert, but she has a rescuer personality. She's married with twin boys and still looking to take care of "lost causes".

"I've always been a church-goer. I think it's important, at least for me, to chip in, to donate my time. I help out with fundraisers, food drives, homeless meals, delivering food to the elderly, things like that. I also volunteer at the animal shelter one day a week.

"I kind of feel like people are basically good, you know? I do the best I can. My boys are seven now and I thought things were going along fairly well. Miles is no trouble at all. His personality is more like mine—he's just a sweet, easy-going boy with a heart for God. He's a helper bunny. But Matthew can be a handful. I'm used to his behavior, but I guess it can be trying on others.

"He's not really a bad kid, it's just that sometimes he'll have these outbursts over something minor, like a kid at school might say something to him and Matthew will shove him. Of course they always say it's Matt's fault. He's got a reputation.

"It's just that he gets frustrated because he can't communicate like the other kids do, so when the teacher steps in, he starts throwing papers or runs out of the room. He's been evaluated and the school knows darned well he suffers from severe social anxiety. He just doesn't have the skills to deal with criticism or humiliation of any kind. If something makes him uncomfortable, he gets aggressive. He feels embarrassed.

"So this week, we got an invitation to a party from one of the kids in their class, but only Miles was invited. The invitation specifically asked that Matthew not attend because he was disruptive. It was all put in very flowery polite terms, but the message was clear. They didn't like my son.

"My first reaction—and remember, I'm not the vindictive type—but my first reaction was 'if Matt's not invited, then they'll both stay home'. Of course I realized this would be unfair to Miles, so my husband took Miles to the party and I stayed home with Matt.

"We were sitting on the couch watching TV and an overwhelming feeling of loneliness came over me. I can't explain it. I thought I was socially connected in every way. I was always doing something at the church or the homeless shelter or the animal shelter, and now I just felt cut out. I wasn't wanted. It was my son who wasn't wanted, but it reflected on me. We were unloved and unwanted. It was like a quiet devastation filled me.

"I just felt bad. I don't know how else to put it. I felt bad for me, for Matt, for Miles, and for my husband. I felt bad for all the people who don't understand, who are unwilling to be kind or go out of their way to accept someone who's different. So what if Matt caused a scene at the party. I wouldn't be the end of the world. I would have apologized and taken him home. No harm done. But they didn't see it that way. So be it. But what could I do?"

Transformative Takeaway

Tonya interacted with people on a daily basis, yet she felt devastatingly lonely over this incident and at a loss for how to adjust her feelings. Even when her husband and son returned from the party, she was unable to shake it off.

It's common for children like Matthew to be troublesome at school where burdens and expectations put a strain on them that they are unable handle. For teachers and staff, it often seems as though this sudden onset behavior comes out of left field, and it can be very confusing. They feel helpless and resort to what they know: discipline, policy, and rules.

But social anxiety is a large part of the problem. Matthew was not equipped with the communication skills it would have taken to avoid this type of confrontation, so he became disruptive as a result of his anxiety. He pushed away the very people who might have helped him be secure. Teachers are often ill-equipped for this as well. So instead of working together—Matthew learning to manage his anxiety and teachers educating themselves on social anxiety disorders in children—kids often spend half the day in the principal's office.

For Tonya, it would be a good idea to talk to some of the other parents or attend a PTA meeting and explain to them that Matthew has trouble with social anxiety, that's it's not anger or opposition. Letting others know *why* he behaves the way he does and offering tools to intervene in her absence might help lower Matthew's threat response.

Betrayal

> "Because no retreat from the world can mask what is in your face." (Gregory Maguire)

Martin is fifty-three years old and has ASD. His parents are elderly and are no longer able to take care of him. He can't do most of the things adults do on their own and needs the care of a group home.

Martin is nonverbal and hyperactive, but on top of all that, he has episodes of self-injurious behavior. He hits his head against the wall, bites, and hits staff members. Because of this, he receives increasingly higher and higher doses of antipsychotic medication in order to subdue him.

"We tried to care for Martin. We did it for fifty years, but I'm in my eighties and so is my husband. It's just too much sometimes. I was beyond myself when the doctor told me he found small bumps on Martin's genitals during a routine prostate exam. I wasn't sure what it meant.

"He told me the only way Martin could have gotten Herpes was through sexual intercourse. But I know he didn't do this on his own. I know it. I'm his mother. Someone in that place took advantage of him. My poor boy. He can't defend himself. And with all those drugs they've been giving him, it was probably easy for some pervert to do it.

"Well my husband was fit to be tied. He drove right over to that place and demanded to speak to the director. I insisted on going with him. Of course they denied any wrong-doing, telling us none of their staff would do such a thing as abuse a resident. They blamed Martin.

"The boy hasn't said a word his entire life, so how could he tell us what happened? I cried all night for him. What he must have gone through and not being able to defend himself. Who knows? There could have been two of them that did it. The world is full of perverts these days. It's sickening.

"Well I had my proof sure enough, but it doesn't mean anything. We were determined to get him out of there. When the orderly took us to Martin's room so we could pack up his things and take him home, he became violent and wouldn't let the man touch him. He was the one, alright. I just gave him the worst look and told him he should be ashamed.

"Since he's been home, he hasn't had any episodes of violence or even bad behavior. He just sits with himself and his things or watches TV or looks at books. We get help from a live-in now. My husband can't bathe him or take care of things, so the aide does most of the work, but at least we're here to see what goes on.

"I feel so guilty, like I **betrayed** him in some way. Like I didn't care enough to keep him home. Fifty years ago, we couldn't have gotten the help we have available today. Doctors just didn't know about these kinds of children. I don't even know if he realizes how much we love him. He has a trust that he'll draw from when we're gone. But I worry all the time about the actual people who will be responsible for his care. The money will be there, but what about good people? I've lived with a broken heart for more than fifty years, and it won't stop until the day I die."

TRANSFORMATIVE TAKEAWAY
This is an all-to-common occurrence in group homes, where residents who can't advocate for themselves are abused and taken advantage of sexually. No one wants to talk about it, but this vulnerable population is at risk for all sorts of neglect. Medication is not always the answer. Often, it's the environment that's causing their behavior, as was the case with Martin. Future planning for your autistic adult-child is necessary to ensure your wishes are carried out in the event of an untimely death. Consulting with a special needs attorney may provide solace and assurance, giving you the peace of mind you deserve.

Exhaustion

> *"Sometimes exhaustion is not a result of too much time spent on something, but of knowing that in its place, no time is spent on something else." (Joyce Rachelle)*

Sonia is in her second marriage. She has four boys between the ages of twelve and six and finds it very difficult to keep up with running a household. In fact, she doesn't like housework at all and takes the kids out to MacDonald's several nights a week. She rarely cooks. It's always frozen pizzas, hot pockets, chips and sodas, and hotdogs. The boys don't mind, but their nutrition—and hers—is likely suffering. She's also a pack-a-day cigarette smoker who curses like a drunken sailor and tends to neglect herself in favor of her boys' needs.

"Garret, my nine-year-old, was up all night. He wanted to watch TV and I kept turning it off. I'd leave the room and he'd turn it back on. Finally, I literally had to unplug the friggin' TV and take it out of the room. Like that was something I really love doing at two in the morning.

"So I go back into the room and he's under the covers like a tent on his iPad. I was ready to hit the ceiling. I took it away from him and he starts crying again. Now it's three o'clock and he's been whining and crying for five hours. I finally just gave up. I knew the next few hours were going to be hell because he had to get up for school.

"My oldest is pretty good about helping out. He made sure the other two were dressed, and Joel was still in bed when the older boys finally got on the bus. But I was so friggin' **exhausted**, I wanted to cry.

"I let Robbie sleep and got into the shower. As soon as the water hit me, the floodgates opened. I couldn't stop crying. I just stood there and let the water run over my face. After about ten minutes, I got out of the shower, but I just wanted to go back to bed and forget about everything.

"My husband wasn't much help. He works the night shift, so he's out of the house by nine-thirty at night and doesn't get in 'til six-thirty in the morning. Then he eats something and goes to sleep until around three in the afternoon. Believe me, four boys are a lot to deal with. It seems like I'm the only one who does anything around here. I feel like I want to sleep for the rest of my life."

TRANSFORMATIVE TAKEAWAY

Most parents of children in the Spectrum are on an emotional roller-coaster. Because of the constant demands of raising a child with ASD, these parents tend to neglect themselves in favor of devoting all their time to their child's needs. And with little to no time to do anything else, they run themselves into exhaustion. Their goal is to keep going until the job is done. But in an overwhelming number of cases, the job will never be done.

Here again, behavioral therapy would help Sonia and Garret reach a new level of understanding that could lead to changes in both their lives. For Sonia, she needed to find time to engage in positive, socially reinforcing activities to gain some perspective on everything she goes through at home.

For Garret, the "if/then" would work. If he turns off the TV and goes to sleep now, he can watch an extra hour of TV tomorrow after school. The use of the timer would also work well here. She could also introduce him to something new, something physical that might better channel his energy so he could sleep at night.

Turn off all electronic devices (phones, computers, TV, iPads, tablets, video games) for at least one hour before bedtime. The blue light from these devices restrains the production of melatonin and interrupts the sleep/wake cycle. Blue wavelengths work well for us during the day because they boost attention and even create better emotional mood, but it works to our disadvantage at night, after the sun goes down.

"While light of any kind can suppress the secretion of melatonin, blue light at night does so more powerfully. Harvard researchers and their colleagues conducted an experiment comparing the effects of 6.5 hours of exposure to blue light to exposure to green light of comparable brightness. The blue light suppressed melatonin for about twice as long as the green light and shifted circadian rhythms by twice as much (3 hours vs. 1.5 hours)." (Harvard, May 2012)

Avoiding bright screens and artificial lights two to three hours before bedtime is ideal, and allowing children to get more natural sunlight will adjust their circadian rhythms and promote sound sleep.

Sonia is also in great need of a healthy diet for herself and her children, particularly Garret. Their diets are high in gluten and artificial additives, which can trigger reactions in certain people. For Garret, at least, it's recommended that Sonia speak to her pediatrician or a dietician who has experience with Spectrum children.

Excitement

"The excitement of dreams coming true is beyond the description of words." (Lailah Gifty Akita)

Patricia is always remembered for her positive energy and easy-going nature. She's a cashier at a convenience store and people seem to gravitate towards her. She's supportive of family and friends and is always the first one to step up and help out. Her ten-year-old daughter, Meghan, is non-verbal. Meghan is very well-behaved and has no issues with tantrums, aggression, or opposition.

"I tend to be overly friendly sometimes. As my sister says, I never met a stranger. I talk to everyone. I'm just chatty. That's why I love my job. I get to see different people all day long.

"It seemed like Meghan always did better when the room was quiet so I had gotten her a noise-cancelling headset to help her out when we went to places where there were a lot of people. So on Saturday, we went to Rivergate [Mall] to get Meghan new shoes and she wore her headset as we walked through the mall. There's a little shop there that sells ice cream, and as we walked past it, Meghan said, "Want ice cream." I nearly hit the ceiling!

"These were literally her first words in ten years! I was beyond ecstatic! Her very first words! Can you imagine how I felt? I wanted to shout to someone, 'my daughter just talked!' I knelt down to meet her and asked her what kind she wanted. I wasn't even sure she knew what was available or that she would continue to talk. She didn't. She just pointed. I'd read that non-verbal children eventually begin to speak, so I was always hopeful of course. But I was happy with what I got for the moment. Happier than I've ever been in my life."

TRANSFORMATIVE TAKEAWAY
We often think of non-verbal children as not being able to understand or respond to verbal information, and there's nothing to

suggest that this is linked in any way to basic intelligence. No one really knows why some children don't talk.

Meghan would be considered pre-verbal at this point. According to an NIH Workshop publication on Nonverbal School-Aged Children with Autism, "...it is a very significant challenge to assess these individuals with traditional standardized instruments. Our current measurement tools have relatively low reliability and validity for this population. The presence of even one word, or some echolalic speech (repeating or echoing the words of others exactly with or without grasping the meaning), appears to be a significant predictor for the acquisition of spoken language after five years of age.

"In both research and treatment planning, it is important to distinguish whether children are nonverbal (no spoken language), preverbal (younger children who have not yet developed verbal language), or non-communicative (having neither verbal nor nonverbal communication skills)." (Kasari, et al, 2010)

Play therapy and speech therapy are two valuable tools Patricia could employ to encourage verbal communication from Meghan.

Part Two

Where Does Your Child Fit In?

"I remember always being baffled by other children. I would be at a birthday party and watch the other kids giggling and making faces, and I would try to do that, too, but I wouldn't understand why. I would sit there with the tight elastic thread of the birthday hat parting the pudge of my under chin, with the grainy frosting of the cake bluing my teeth, and I would try to figure out why it was fun." (Gillian Flynn, *Gone Girl*)

THE THREE TYPES OF AUTISM SPECTRUM DISORDERS

Not all autism is the same. The Autism Spectrum is so-called because it covers a wide range of complex disorders in brain development. In 2013, the criteria for an autism diagnosis was changed in order to combine all types of autism under one category (NIMH, 2019). In efforts to understand the range of cognitive abilities, this section will simplify the guidelines from the *Diagnostic and Statistical Manual of Mental Disorders* (DSM) (APA, 2000). There are three basic types of autism: Classic Autistic Disorder, Asperger's Syndrome, and Pervasive Developmental Disorder.

CLASSIC AUTISM

This is the type that most people think of when they hear the word *autism*. Symptoms include significant language delays, non-verbal or verbal communication challenges, social challenges, and unusual behaviors and interests. This is the most common type.

These children (or adults or teens) may have a problem with being touched by others. They often perform repetitive behaviors and can easily experience sensory overload. These symptoms can be found in other types of autism, but in "classic" patients, they tend to be more severe.

Asperger's Syndrome

Asperger's is a less severe form of classic autism, with many of the same symptoms. These individuals exhibit unusual behaviors and don't have as many problems with language or intellectual disability, but they experience social challenges, which seems to be their greatest challenge.

Pervasive Developmental Disorder- Not Otherwise Specified (PDD-NOS)

These children are atypical. They don't meet all the criteria for either Classic or Asperger's, but they do meet some. Their symptoms are usually milder and fewer. Often, their challenges are only social and/or communicative. They are generally high-functioning autistic types.

WHAT THEY DIDN'T EXPECT

"What I have since realized is that if people expect you to be brave, sometimes you pretend that you are, even when you are frightened down to your very bones." (Sharon Creech, *Walk Two Moons*)

Your doctor will tell you about where your child fits into the Spectrum and about all the symptoms, some of which you may have already noticed. This may be why you brought your child in to begin with. Your child may be experiencing some of these symptoms, but ASD affects every person differently. Two people diagnosed with the same type or category of autism, even within the same family, may exhibit different symptoms, which can vary from mild to severe.

The American Autism Association is a valuable resource with an abundance of information, and is available to anyone in need of further learning. (See *Resources* at the end of this book).

- Poor/No Eye Contact
- Non-Responsiveness
- No Communication
- Non-Verbal Communication
- Social Anxiety
- Repetitive or Odd Behaviors
- Poor Motor Skills
- Tuning Out
- Wandering
- Temper Tantrums
- No Pretend Play
- Attachment to Hard Inanimate Objects

These are Their Stories

"In order to complete our amazing life journey successfully, it is vital that we turn each and every dark tear into a pearl of wisdom, and find the blessing in every curse." (Anthon St. Maarten, *Divine Living: The Essential Guide to Your True Destiny*)

Some of the following stories are continuations of the people you've already met in Part One, and some are new. These are the stories of ordinary people who are going through their lives just like you, and their reactions to the triggers that caused the event. You may find yourself in one or more of their situations.

Poor/No Eye Contact

"Listen to the mustn'ts, child. Listen to the don'ts. Listen to the shouldn'ts, the impossibles, the won'ts. Listen to the never haves, then listen close to me... Anything can happen, child. Anything can be." (Shel Silverstein)

Beryl and Will couldn't have children and made plans to adopt. When they first met Hannah, the three-year-old girl who would be their new daughter, they immediately noticed she was not walking or talking.

Beryl: "She cried, she struggled really hard to get away from me. They told me she was never picked up and held. She just didn't like it so they usually left her on the floor to play.

"After several months, I had Hannah evaluated for autism. Her behaviors, head-banging and an inability to talk or even walk well, and the fact that she made absolutely no eye contact with me or Will concerned me quite a bit. She was diagnosed with autism.

"We didn't sign on for this, but we really loved this little girl, and now I'm very happy we stuck it out. We take her to occupational therapy, speech therapy, and to a special camp where she gets horseback riding therapy. Our community has a special needs kindergarten with personal one-on-one care.

"Hannah has turned out to have a very sweet nature. I don't know if this would have ever been brought out of her had she remained in the orphanage. Will just loves her to death.

"Of course, we're not there yet. In a few weeks, she'll be going into a two-week intensive toilet training program at the Marcus Autism Center. They have a very good success rate. She still has to wear a helmet at school, but the head-banging is less frequent."

Will: "Through all of this, I didn't feel like we really had to give up a lot. I work from home, so I was able to help a lot. Beryl didn't have to do it all herself. When we go out, we just plan for places where there's not going to be any complications or triggers that might confuse Hannah. We manage to have fun. We do most of the same things any parents with children do. It's just that we do it a bit differently, that's all. Our friends have been really supportive. We do invite them over, just not all at once.

"I don't think most of them really understand the struggle. And there is one, but I don't see it as necessarily a really bad thing. You know how people ask 'how are you' and it's just a polite phrase? I'll generally just say I'm good or we're good. But I have one friend who insisted on knowing how I was really doing. He said he had no idea of what I might be going through, so I told him. It was a great relief just to be able to talk to someone who wasn't a therapist. (Laughs).

"I think we all need friends who are understanding and supportive. I'm not asking anyone to take my burden or even share it. Just to be open and understanding. To visit now and then and act normal.

"I've grown in a profound way. This morning Hannah looked me straight in the eye and leaned in for a kiss. I rejoice more in small moments of surprise."

People who don't make eye contact might just be shy, introverted, intimidated, or inhibited in some other way, but not making eye contact is a very common trait among autistic children and adults. They're uncomfortable making eye contact for a number of potential reasons.

- They don't see the value in it yet.
- They're so distracted by something else that they don't want to break away. They're disinterested or not paying attention.
- They may think that by not looking at you, you can't see them. They prefer not to be noticed, not to be the center of attention.
- They don't 'notice' or acknowledge you, meaning you're not important at that moment.

It is difficult for some autistic children to express their thoughts, so the reasons for the lack of eye contact may vary. But once you are able to get your child to just glance in your direction, you're on the right path to eventually developing better eye contact—at least occasionally.

Non-Responsiveness

> *"Wellness is not a 'medical fix' but a way of living - a lifestyle sensitive and responsive to all the dimensions of body, mind, and spirit, an approach to life we each design."* (Greg Anderson)

Sandy is the over-achiever we met earlier, the nurse who experienced shock and disbelief when her son, James, was given the diagnosis of autism. She had brought him in because he was unnaturally unresponsive to his name and to visual cues and sounds.

"Once I got over the shock of the diagnosis, and after I'd changed pediatricians four times, I began to pay more attention to James's behavior. I looked for patterns. For me, it wasn't a matter if disciplining bad behavior, it was a matter of learning to respond to unresponsiveness. Learning to deal with it in a productive healthy way that might help James and my understanding of him.

"He didn't even look up when I called his name. I needed to know that I was at least connecting to him in some way. He was already three now and I didn't know if this unresponsive behavior was due to something he couldn't do or just wouldn't do. So the first thing I tried was the reward system. He loved getting tickled, so every time I called his name, I would then walk over and tickle him. He would laugh.

"The next time, I would call his name while standing in front of him. When he didn't respond, I bent down to his eye level and put up my "tickle" hands, wiggling my fingers like I was going to tickle him. Then I stood up and called his name again. I repeated this a few times until he made the association with his name and tickling. It actually worked. I was happy to learn that he *could* respond when he wanted to, when there was something he wanted. He still didn't make eye contact, but at least I had made some progress. I knew he was actually in there."

James didn't see value in merely responding to his name. To him, there was no point. But when he associated it with the reward of being tickled, he found it to have value to him. In other words, he was motivated to respond because he was going to get something he enjoyed.

Building skills for name response

Family involvement is critical in helping autistic children build life skills. Here are some strategies for dealing with unresponsiveness. They're simple and parents can try them at home.

1. First find an opportunity when your child is not deeply involved in something like TV or a video game. They may be mildly occupied with another activity. This is the time to approach him or her.

2. Say his name then immediately tap him on the shoulder to reinforce the association. You can also gently lift his head to face you. Don't expect or require direct eye contact just yet as it can be uncomfortable for this type of child.
3. As soon as your child looks towards you, reward him with a toy, hug, or other activity, like Sandra did with tickling. This was something her son enjoyed and it worked for her. Praise your child for responding. Then let him go back to whatever he was doing before.

You could potentially repeat these steps 10 to 20 times or more each day if you have the time. If you only have a little time, practice with one or two minutes in between each time you call his name.

James was excited the first few times Sandra tickled him, but became tired or bored with it. If you notice a decrease in enjoyment or excitement, give your child a break. And keep in mind that some children need more practice than others.

If this doesn't work well at the start and you've been at it for an hour, check your surroundings. Are there distractions that are competing for your child's attention such as TV, music, other children playing or making noise or playing video games in the room?

Eventually you'll need to expand your child's circle for this practice to other people and places. When your child responds to his or her name without you having to use physical cues like tapping him on the shoulder or guiding his face to look at you, he or she is ready to expand.

1. Do the same thing you've been doing, only try it in a different place: a different room, outside, or in the car. Remember to praise and reward even the slightest look in your direction.
2. Include other people, at the dinner table for example. Only do this with people you trust. You can call his name (al-

ways praising and rewarding) or family members can do it. Don't, however, overwhelm the child by having more than one person at a time call his name. The idea is to have your child respond to his name with as many people and in as many places as possible.
3. At some point, when he is responding consistently to you and other people calling his name in various places, increase the distance between the two of you. Go from a few feet away to across the room to across the yard, but always stay within a safe range.

No Communication

"You can talk with someone for years, every day, and still it won't mean as much as what you can have when you sit in front of someone, not saying a word, yet you feel that person with your heart." (C. JoyBell C.)

Janet is the mother of four boys, ages eleven, nine, six, and three. Her first three boys grew and developed at the standard expected rate, but with her youngest, Brady, she began to notice he was doing things differently.

"The first thing I noticed—and I didn't really catch on to it right away—was that he wasn't showing any interest in the things babies normally react to like my first three did. He didn't follow the sound of my voice or my husband's or the other boys' voices when they came in to play with him in his crib. It seemed like he wasn't listening at all. My first thought was that maybe he had a hearing problem, or his hearing wasn't developed yet. I didn't even know if this was a thing. But I noticed he didn't even look at me or do the usual baby-babbling.

"The other boys all started talking when they were around one. Well not really talking, just a few words, a couple of words here and there. They were really just imitating what I was saying and picking up a word. But eventually they started to put the words together.

"With Brady, there was nothing. Not even a babble. And he was almost two. I still thought maybe he was born deaf or something, but wouldn't even a deaf baby look around? Wouldn't he look at his mother when she picked him up? I kind of started to feel nervous about this. The pediatrician never mentioned anything about anything regarding this. And I never asked because I really didn't know.

"I took him for regular pediatric exams, but they really only look at kids for twenty minutes. They do vaccinations, and check overall head to toe, but no one said anything to me about this. I really started to worry when Brady was three and still not talking, so I had his hearing checked. They put the headphones on him and he responded to the sounds with a jump, like he was startled. He even looked in the direction he thought it was coming from. The diagnosis was that his hearing 'seemed to be okay' and I should wait three to six months and have him checked again. It never occurred to me that he could be autistic. After all, I had three other kids who were normal."

"When my sister asked me if Brady had been evaluated for autism, I nearly hit the floor! It was something I knew nothing about and didn't want to know. Maybe I was in denial. But the thought kept nagging at me for weeks and I finally did get him evaluated and the diagnosis was classic autism—non-communicative. At least up to this point. I was assured that with intervention and therapy, there was hope Brady might improve."

Unfortunately, pediatricians can miss signs and symptoms of autism in the brief time it takes to give a child a general check-up. Although speech delays are common in many children and are not always due to autism, there are differences between autistic and non-autistic children.

Typical children learn that language gets them what they want, even if it's only crying. They're motivated by sounds and imitate the speech of those around them. They tend to not like being left alone. Autistic children are more inclined to be interested in things, not people, and tend to want their own company. They also don't make the connection that even non-verbal actions like pointing or smiling can get them what they want.

If your child has delayed communication skills, look for these early signs of autism:

- Failure to respond to his or her name
- Does not use gestures
- Uses pictures to communicate or makes up their own sign language
- Uses only single words and/or repeats single words or phrases, but seems unable to make sentences
- Echoes words without seeming to understand their meaning
- Uses words that are out of context and have no meaning to anyone but those who are familiar with the child

In a Brigham Young University study, "referrals for thirty-nine percent of study subjects (children with autism) were missed, based on the brief observation alone." (Miller, et al., 2015) Janet's pediatrician, though well meaning, may have been leading her down a wrong path. Although nearly thirty-five percent of those on the autism spectrum use no spoken language, we just don't know enough about their thought processes.

Brady may eventually speak a few words. Janet drives a pickup truck, so he might say a word such as 'truck' to let Janet know he wants to go for a ride, but he would not be able to tell her where he wants to go, even if asked that direct question. But speech and communication are not the same thing. Though Brady may or may not remain non-verbal, he may learn to communicate in other ways.

Non-Verbal Communication

"The most important thing in communication is hearing what isn't said." (Peter Drucker)

Do you remember Patricia? She's the upbeat mother of ten-year-old Meghan who spoke her very first words in front of an ice cream shop at the mall.

"Before that day, Meghan managed to communicate by pointing at something or pulling me toward what she wanted. If I didn't understand, she would take a stance with her feet apart and her hands on her hips and look at me. This is something I do and she would use the imitation as if to say, 'Are you dense? Why aren't you understanding me?' Generally, she managed to get her point across. But her inability to actually talk—or her unwillingness to do so—left a kind of void in my life. I just wanted to hear my daughter's thoughts.

"After the day at the mall, about two weeks later, she was watching Curious George on TV. We all know George is a respectful and very resourceful little monkey, and the man with the yellow hat is okay, too. Hey, he's got a monkey for a kid. How bad can the guy be, right? I was in the kitchen getting dinner ready when Meghan walked in and said 'hat'. I heard it, but I wasn't sure what I heard.

"I stopped what I was doing and looked at her. 'Hat'. She actually did not own a hat of any kind, so I was a bit baffled. I thought about it for a moment, not relating it to George in any way at all. I had a straw sun hat, a blue sun visor, and a slouchy, yellow-vinyl mushroom hat that went with an old raincoat. I don't wear it much unless we're in a downpour, and then I mostly only throw it on to run out to get the mail or something. I don't know that she's ever even seen it. I took her upstairs and pulled out all three of my hats, the only three I had. I also pulled out my husband's Yankees baseball cap and laid them all on the bed.

"'Hat'. She instantly pointed to the yellow hat. Hmmm. I didn't know what to make of it, but I was okay with another word, even though to me it seemed out of context to anything. I let her take the hat and she put it on her head, wearing it around the house for the rest of the day. The next day, same time—Curious George time—I watched her bring the hat into the living room and turn on the TV. She put the hat on her head and began to watch Curious George.

"Oh... hat! I got it."

Research is showing that non-verbal children can learn to speak at any age, so language development should be an important part of your development plan. Although Meghan was able to 'get her point across', it seems that she learned with the first word that words are effective, so she tried another. But each child will be different.

Associating gestures with words

Here are a few strategies that will help you communicate with your child and give him or her the opportunity to associate gestures with words.

- **Try imitating any sounds your child makes.** This will encourage him or her to imitate sounds you make (words). If a child gets what he wants by pointing, always say the word associated with that item or desire. And make sure to do so at eye level so you're sure they're paying attention.
- **Silence can be golden.** Don't feel you have to fill in every moment with talking or words. Give your child a chance to respond. Chances are good he or she is thinking about it. As is the case with many autistic children, they won't compete for social space; they won't talk over you (unless they're experiencing a meltdown), and they likely won't grasp as much if your give them too much at once. Keep it simple.

- **Up the ante.** If your child is able to communicate with single words, as eventually happened with Meghan, speak to him or her with double words. For example, when Meghan wanted the hat, Patricia could have said 'yellow hat'. Of course, at that point Meghan wasn't ready, but you get the point.

There are several devices and apps available that will produce a word when your child touches a picture. These and many other types of supports can aide in developing speech. (See *Resources*)

Social Anxiety

> *"All I feel are the assaults of apprehension and terror at the thought that I am the only one who is entirely unlike the rest."*
> (Osamu Dazai, *No Longer Human*)

You might remember Jeff, the single father of two boys. His seven-year-old, Jacob (Jake) had stuffed Jeff's friend's toilet with paper, and Jeff was feeling very frustrated.

"Marc told me not to worry about it. He'd take care of it, No harm done. But I was feeling awkward. I'm not really a sociable person. It's not that I don't like people, I just don't feel like I fit in anywhere. I'll go out with friends and pretty much just sit there and watch everyone else having what they call fun. Drinking beers and watching sports.

"I've noticed recently that my oldest, Josh, he's twelve, might be having a similar problem. He doesn't ever want to go to birthday parties or outings. Even at school, he fights against going on field trips. But it's part of the curriculum and he has to go. He says he just doesn't have fun. It's boring. The other kids are 'boring' or 'stupid'.

"He likes to entertain himself. I used to think he was just a loner, which was okay with me because I'm a bit of a loner. But I think kids should be out having fun, doing things with other kids. He goes out of his way to avoid interaction with schoolmates. Actually with people in general. Could it be just that he's preteen?

"But he doesn't talk on the phone with friends. That would be a typical thing for a kid his age. There's a kid up the block who comes over once a week or so and they get along well. I just don't know. I don't really want to have him checked for autism. I don't want him to have that stigma, but on the other hand, I've spent many a New Year's Eve alone before I got married and I don't want him to go through life like I did, afraid of talking to people and being alone most of the time."

This is an age where it might be difficult to determine whether or not a person is autistic in some form; whether their behavior is part of the Spectrum developmental disorders or he's just going through growing pains.

If this is your child, think about when this type of loner behavior began. Were they always like this? Or did it begin in Middle School when children are often subjected to peer pressure. If you can get your preteen to open up about something that may have happened that triggered this behavior, you can possibly work through it.

For Jeff, he began to quietly listen to Josh's conversations with his friend when he came over. They usually retreated to Josh's room or sat outside on the back deck. It seemed to Jeff that the conversations were normal healthy boy-talk, so Jeff dismissed having him evaluated for social anxiety.

There is a real concern for those with social anxiety. This is something that can develop over time and goes beyond a lack of social skills. Avoidance of social stimuli and situations perceived as potentially threatening, though they are not, can inhibit adult success in job seeking, maintaining a job, relationships, and general personal growth potential.

Because autism spectrum disorder and social anxiety disorder have partly overlapping symptoms in the areas of social interaction and social skills, there are no clear-cut borderlines. Consult with your child's health provider for more clarity.

Repetitive or Odd Behaviors

> *"You are a marvel. You are unique. In all the years that have passed, there has never been another child like you. Your legs, your arms, your clever fingers, the way you move. You may become a Shakespeare, a Michelangelo, a Beethoven. You have the capacity for anything."* (Henry David Thoreau)

Retired Command Sergeant Major John couldn't understand his son, John Jr's, repetitive behaviors. JJ would fixate on his Matchbox cars, lining them up in a very specific order, by color and with precision spacing between each car.

"It's amazing to watch. He'll literally sit there for hours lining up these cars. He might pick one up and inspect it for a minute, pretend to race it, then line it back up again. I've seen him make patterns with them. All the reds together, all the blues together, or every other color in a specific order. He'll make circles, lines, stars, boxes, you name it. But it's always with precision accuracy.

"So now I'm thinking, if he can do this—this precision thing— I might be able to use that and apply it to something else, like eating. So I planned the next meal with my wife and told her my plan. I was going to use colorful food and group them together in a pattern like a star just to see his reaction.

"When he sat down to eat, he took some time studying the plate. On it were baby carrots, three grilled chicken strips, and three broccoli florets. I made a small star from ten baby carrots. I lined the chicken strips up north-south inside the star and put a broccoli floret at the top and two side points.

"My wife and I watched him, looked at each other, and couldn't keep from smiling. What was he doing? What was he thinking? After about three minutes, with JJ looking intently at his plate, his eyes were almost twitching with intelligent thought. Suddenly he took the chicken out of the center and carefully replaced it with the broccoli so that they formed a mound with the heads up. He placed the chicken at the top point, facing east west. The world made sense to him again.

"But he ate all the food. Each time he ate something he had to rearrange it. So first went two carrots and the star was made into an octagon, then a hexagon, then a box. Then he ate the broccoli and placed the chicken into the box, north south. It was amazing to watch as each bite turned into some new shape, until the last bite of chicken, with everything else gone, was placed in the direct center of the plate. He looked at it for a long time and finally ate it. Hmmm."

Retraining and exposure to new things, ideas, and possibilities is at the core of teaching autistic children who are capable of learning. Once again, John was on the right track. Instead of trying to break JJ of his repetitive behavioral patterns, which in JJ's case were essentially harmless, he used them to give JJ a new way of looking at food which resulted in less fuss about actually eating it.

Ideally, you will want to introduce some behavioral modification to your child's repetitive behavior. Reward your child for gradually accepting small changes. For JJ, he might be rewarded in some way by allowing John to place a car or two out of order, at least for a few minutes. This type of behavior, lining things up, is common and can be used as another type of learning tool. Counting is the obvious example, but what if John were to assign a letter, name, or word to each of JJ's cars? He could potentially learn to count, arrange letters into words and words into sentences.

More research needs to be done into behavioral interventions. Early intervention may help make change and flexibility easier for the child.

Poor Motor Skills

"When someone is nasty or treats you poorly, don't take it personally. It says nothing about you, but a lot about them."
(Michael Josephson)

"Mandy is the mother of nine-year-old Zach who was just recently diagnosed with Asperger's.

"He was very clumsy for a boy his age. I thought it was just because he was a clumsy boy. But he consistently dropped things and broke glasses because they slipped out of his hands. He stumbled a lot and walked like an old man, sort of moving his feet parallel to each other instead of one in front of the other. When he was younger, we'd throw the ball back and forth and he would never catch it. Sometimes you think your kid is just uncoordinated. No big deal. When he started falling down stairs, I became concerned. I have to admit, I was more than a little scared.

"We were at a school softball game where all kids played regardless of their skill level. I knew Zach wasn't very good at catching or throwing a ball, but this was a kid's game. No score, no real competition. I was set to enjoy a fun hour. But what I got was heart-breaking. The other boys were calling him names. Zach the Hack. Loser. Slippery Fingers. They weren't kidding around either. It was malicious. But Zach did his best.

"On the way home from the game, I asked him if he had fun. 'No.' 'Why not?' 'You heard them. They all hate me. I can't do anything right!' He was practically yelling and started crying in the car. 'Mom, what's wrong with me?'

"It took all my strength to hold myself together. We stopped for ice cream and I told him there might be something we could find out. I suggested we go see the pediatrician and ask a lot of questions. At least this made him feel better for the moment.

"Well, we did go to the doctor. The first thing that came to light was that Zach needed to wear glasses. This helped him at least a little with playing ball. At least he could see it coming. The doctor ruled out MS and MD. He also referred us to a physical therapist and an occupational therapist, which we're doing right now.

"I feel like he's made some improvement. He seems to focus more on the things he had trouble with before, and he'll do things like holding onto the handrail on stairs, and carrying a glass with two hands. He works at the therapist's with puzzles, balls, and building his strength with weights. All supervised of course.

"I'm so happy for him. I look at him now and want to cry because I'm so happy. He's a very changed little boy. He may never be a great softball player, but at least he has more self-esteem and it shows. He's very proud of himself. And that makes a mother proud, too."

Zach has been seeing an occupational therapist to strengthen his fine motor skills—things like using scissors, holding a pencil or silverware, and improving handwriting. His gross motor skills, those things that involve using the larger muscles of the body, are being assisted by his physical therapist. There he will receive help with coordinating both sides of his body and his balance. They often use balls in physical therapy, and in Zach's case, this worked well for him, not only to build his skills but to build his self-esteem.

Tuning Out

> *"People have a problem with me being different, but that propels me forward in life."* (Mary-Louise Parker)

You should remember Denise, the banker by day and wannabe rock star by night. Her daughter Melanie is the beautiful little girl who imitated her mother's pink hair by smearing pink icing in her own hair.

"Ever since that day (referring to the day only three people showed up at Melanie's birthday party) I've been focusing my life on Melanie. I did anyway, but now it was like an intensive program, just me and her. Her behavior wasn't good. That's supposedly why no one showed up, and we've been working on that.

"My biggest problem with her was that she would just tune out from everything. How could I communicate with her or try to teach her anything if she just tuned out all the time? I mean, I know she's in there, she knows what's going on. If she didn't, she wouldn't have put the icing in her hair. I don't know if she understands it, but she knows.

"The day of the party, after the party, we just sat on the couch together. I ate cupcakes, Melanie played with her doll, seemingly oblivious to me and my tears after that initial contact. I tried to recapture the laughter and joy I felt when she handed me the cupcake and I noticed the icing in her hair, and it made me smile. Later that night, I was tucking her into bed and started reading her a story, something we did every night for fifteen minutes. Out of nowhere, Melanie reached over and took the book out of my hands. 'You don't want to read tonight?' I asked her, not really expecting any response. Generally I read, she ignored me. Or at least that's the way it seemed. 'Happy birthday,' she said to her doll, not to me. She was looking at the doll and saying happy birthday over and over.

"She didn't say a word for two months after that, but I was determined to work on it. It's been six months and she muttered two more words—*dolly* and *book*. But I know she's processing. Maybe someday..."

Denise worked hard with Melanie for more than a year teaching her name recognition. She now makes sure Melanie is paying attention, or at least looking at her before she asks a question or reads to her. She uses Melanie's doll as a tool for getting her to pay attention by asking the doll questions about Melanie, simple things like *what does Melanie want to wear today?* Eventually Melanie started going to the closet and picking out clothes. They were often mismatched but Denise went with it.

The key to this method—using Melanie's special interest, her doll—or any other when dealing with non-responsive or non-verbal children is to speak slowly and say less.

- Don't give them too much information to process at one time.
- Don't ask too many questions. If you do ask questions, make it something they understand and can potentially respond to.

In Melanie's case, she was interested in fashion, if you want to call it that, as exemplified by her imitating her mother's hair, so she was able to put the concept of picking out clothes together.

- Use visual supports. Denise could have used doll clothes or paper dolls.
- Be aware of the environment.
- Be very clear and specific with what you say. Don't use sarcasm, irony, or figurative language.

Wandering

"Not all those who wander are lost…" (J.R.R. Tolkien, *The Fellowship of the Ring*)

You'll remember Morgan, the father of the six-year-old boy, Matt, who jumped out of the car on a busy street and proceeded to make his way to the candy shop half a mile away. In a panic, Morgan was confused as to what he should do. Should he just leave his car in traffic and go after Matt, or should he try to pull off the road and then go after him? Doing that, he felt, would cause him to lose valuable time.

"This was all new to me. I had no life skills for this. And going into panic mode wasn't helping me think clearly. It was like I was having a full-blown fight-or-flight response—heart racing, sweating, trembling, heightened senses—all of it. I didn't even want to slow down long enough to talk to the cop, to tell him what had happened, but I had to. And all the time, in the back of my mind, I'm thinking Matt is getting farther and farther away, maybe even picked up by some stranger, or worse. I didn't want to think about it.

"When my wife called me on my cell, it didn't help the situation. I felt like this was my fault. What was I gonna tell her? I lost our kid?

"As it turned out, he'd done this before. He's never jumped out of the car, but Julie told me he had wandered off in the mall. She said he just disappeared. She had barely turned her back on him when he was just gone, and she told me she had that same feeling of heart-in-throat panic. Fortunately, he was only a few feet away, but in the crowded mall, she couldn't spot his little body right away, hidden as it was by all the adults milling around. She didn't want to tell me at the time because she didn't want me to worry.

"It had happened again in the supermarket where he was found in the candy aisle. At the mall, he was just looking in a window of a big-name toy store that had colored balloons as part of their visual display.

"All I know is that it was the most terrifying experience of my life. Seriously. The worst. And I can promise you I will do my due diligence. I don't ever want to feel that again. He literally bolted out and left the car door open! And it's not just for me. What if something worse happened next time? I was planning for 'next time' to never happen."

It's not unusual for children on the Spectrum to wander. It's an impulsive action and can be a huge safety issue that could easily end up being tragic. As these children get older, even as young as three or four, they may learn to unlock doors leading to the outside. Even a deadbolt placed at the top of the door can be accessed using a chair.

Install a loud chime that will alert you every time an outside door is opened. Make this an urgent priority. Some autistic children have been found drowned in creeks or ponds close to the house, or have had very close calls by wandering into traffic.

According to the first major study on wandering conducted by the Interactive Autism Network (IAN), "…roughly fifty percent of children between the ages of four and ten with an ASD wander at some point, four times more than their unaffected siblings. The behavior peaks at four, but almost thirty percent of kids with an ASD between the ages of seven and ten are still eloping, eight times more than their unaffected brothers and sisters.

"Nearly half of the respondents said a child had been missing long enough to cause significant safety concerns, with thirty-two percent calling the police. Two out of three reported their wandering child had a "close call" with a traffic injury, while almost a third said their child had a "close call" with drowning. Another alarming statistic: thirty-five percent of families with wanderers reported their child is "never" or "rarely" able to communicate his name, address or phone number, either verbally or by writing or typing." (Law & Anderson, 2011)

Even high-functioning children can be a flight risk. They become so fixated on their goal—whatever it is that caused them to bolt—that they're unable to respond with the information professionals need to help them, like giving their name or address.

What motivates a child to wander?

> *"Around here... we keep moving, opening up doors and doing new things because we're curious... and curiosity keeps leading us down new paths."* (Walt Disney)

It can be a number of things. Children in general like to explore, and at a young age have no sense of danger. The child may simply recall a place he or she liked and is returning to enjoy it.

When a child is fascinated by something, such as trucks or trains or the color red, he may just be headed for that special interest. If he can hear a train in the distance near your home, he'll head there. Or out to the highway looking for trucks. Or, as was the case with Matt, he just liked the color red, so the storefront with the balloons and the candy stores had plenty of red for him to gaze at. He was just counting the red jelly beans in the big jar.

On the flip side, a child may be trying to get away from something that's making him anxious, like loud voices, arguing, teachers' demands and school stressors, other kids, or something else in his environment that is a trigger for stress. Even a teacher's perfume can be an issue.

If you have a child who wanders (also referred to as elopement), determine if he or she is running away from something or running to something. Your child is at greater risk for harm when he's running away from a situation that's causing stress or anxiety. But don't rule out the dangers of a child running to a favorite spot.

Nadine is the mother of eleven-year-old Joy, a child with Asperger's. Joy had not previously been known to be a flight risk. She was a well-behaved child, not prone to meltdowns or anxiety, and was a communicative nature-lover who liked to take pictures. Joy could spend hours perusing the hundreds of images she'd taken, simply reliving the experience of being around birds, plants, trees, foxes, squirrels, and insects. She was quite good at cropping and enhancing her images on the computer.

"Joy went out for a bike ride on Saturday. It's something we felt comfortable letting her do. We'd never had a problem with this. She always came back in thirty minutes. This was something we learned to do with her. We set her cell phone's timer to twenty-five minutes to alert her and she then would have five minutes to make her way home.

"When forty-five minutes had gone by, I started to worry. I wasn't about to wait longer. There are a lot of trails around where we live, and I always made sure I watched which trail she went down when she left the house. I tried not to panic and called my husband downstairs to come with me to look for her.

"What we found was beyond our wildest hallucinations. I'd lost many a night's sleep when she was younger worrying if she was going to escape during the night, but nothing had prepared my for the imminent danger we found surrounding Joy when we finally came across her bike on the path.

"I could hear the camera clicks and I could hear her talking in a sing-song voice. We followed the sounds through a thick clump of trees. Joy was standing waist deep in a swamp taking pictures of the wildlife around her. Two young alligators were eyeing her as she stood there talking to them and taking their picture.

"My heart stopped and my voice caught in my throat. I didn't want to make a sound. Rob quietly walked back to the trail and called 911.

"'Hi, Mommy. Look at these guys.' She was the picture of innocence waiting to be devoured. I'm not sure why she wasn't being attacked, but she just walked out of the swamp to show me the pictures she'd taken and the alligators sank below the surface.

"I don't know if I believe in the hand of God, but I do know this: something protects children and idiots. Everyone arrived at the same time—police, paramedics, animal control—and they were armed. But a crisis was averted. And like something out of the mouths of babes, Joy just took their picture."

For Joy, she had no fear of something we would see as dangerous and therefore be afraid of. But the reverse is also true for these children who are afraid of things we would not consider dangerous.

Some parents won't be as lucky as Nadine and Rob. A new diagnostic code for wandering has been added which classifies this behavior in conjunction with other diagnostic codes. This will help pediatricians gather information and create a better understanding of this trait. It's hoped that this new awareness will open the door for more funding for research and training for first responders, particularly regarding those children who are non-communicative or who may feel threatened.

The reverse is also true here. A teen who is attracted to a shiny badge or a nightstick might reach for it. This is not unusual, but a police officer might feel threatened and make a wrong decision that might end up in injury to the child. It may be necessary to take extra precautions to ensure your child's safety.

- Water-related fatalities are significant. One theory is that water may have a calming effect, perhaps because of the repetitive nature of waves and ripples or the sensory feel on the body. Equipping your child with a water-proof tracking device may expedite the search efforts and prevent a potential tragedy.

- Putting an alarm on your child's phone will alert high-functioning children when it's time to go home.
- Door and window alarms may prevent escapes and allow you to get much-needed sleep.
- Place an ID wrist band on children who have limited verbal skills.
- If you place your child in daycare or school, request a 1:1 aide for your child's IEP (Individualized Education Plan). The aide will stay with your child during all transitions.

Temper Tantrums and Sensory Meltdowns

"Maybe we swore we would never be harsh with our children. Then, just when they need us most - when they act up and misbehave and call us names, we get angry and punish them, or feel hurt and block them out. We momentarily forget how fragile our little ones are." (Lawrence J. Cohen, *Playful Parenting*)

Jennifer is the mother of four whose son, Marcus, was thrown out of an expensive daycare facility due to his disruptive behavior. She was extremely angry when it happened, and Marcus has now been diagnosed with ASD. She's since tried to understand that this type of behavior—temper tantrums—can have a very disturbing effect on the rest of the children and on the curriculum of the center. Teachers—particularly daycare providers—are generally ill-equipped to handle this. And many schools maintain a zero-tolerance policy.

"I'm on my own here. It's just me, the dog, and the kids. I have a lot on my plate as it is with four of them, and Marcus's tantrums aren't helping. My anger has subsided for the most part. Now I concentrate on trying to keep things running smoothly around here. I'm not bitter anymore. I know it's up to me to make this right. I spent a few years in denial, but now it's me and my kids against the world. And I'm determined. Sometimes, though, I still get mad. Like why did this have to happen to him?

"When we're out and he's behaving badly, I get all kinds of looks like 'this kid is spoiled rotten' or 'can't you shut that kid up?'. I know what they're thinking and I want to walk around with a sticky note on his forehead that says "he's autistic".

"Every so often, maybe once a week, he has a meltdown. It used to be every day, but it was my oldest boy who hit on a possible reason for the fits. He noticed that Marcus always seemed to have a tantrum when there was a lot going on, like all the boys were play fighting, or all the electronics were on at the same time: TV, video game, and my daughter practicing her flute-a-phone. It was like he went into some kind of sensory overload or something.

"But on the days or at times when things were really calm, like the other kids were out at some extracurricular activity, he was fine. I mean really fine. This is probably what was going on at the daycare center—too many kids around him all at once doing all kinds of activities. He just couldn't handle it.

"I make a point to not have all those things going on at once, at least at home where I can control it. We don't give him any big social challenges, like field trips at school. There's no way I'm subjecting him to that. We might go to the Science Center, but I always do it on a school day, when there won't be a lot of other kids and parents there. I'm learning. I just hope he can outgrow it so he can lead a somewhat normal life when he gets older."

Jennifer was lucky to have worked out part of the problem on her own with the help of her older son, but many parents aren't that lucky. They spend years trying to reason through tantrums as they're occurring. This just doesn't work because at that moment, reason doesn't exist for the child. So what should you do? First of all, learn to recognize triggers, as Jennifer did with the sensory overload her son was experiencing, then avoid them as much as possible.

Dealing with tantrums and meltdowns

At some point, many parents will deal with a temper tantrum or meltdown, and they can be extremely frightening for you. You feel helpless and at a loss for what to do. On top of that, there's often the pressure and stress of being in a public place and you will naturally feel self-conscious and embarrassed. You'll have to live through it and learn the best way to deal with these situations according to your own child's particular triggers.

Sometimes parents think they are calming the child down but instead they escalate the problem with constant nagging. ASD kids are very sensible. They recognize energies. They are very intuitive and often feed off the energy of others. When parents are yelling they will yell and continue the tantrum. Yelling and nagging can actually trigger tantrums.

With my son, Wes, I learned to use a very soft voice when he was going through a tantrum. I wanted him to learn how to express himself without having a meltdown. He is very calm now and independent, but I had to learn the hard way, something many parents do.

During my era, we didn't have nearly as many resources as parents have available to them today. So I learned to adjust to his learning style while introducing him to my world. I learned to embrace his world and he is welcoming my world. The perfect synergy.

1. **Remain calm.** When it's actually happening, you want to remain calm. This is critical. Emotions are contagious and your child will quickly reflect what you're feeling/projecting.

2. **Create a diversion.** Say something funny, laugh, and use anything you have in your arsenal that will take your child's attention elsewhere. If you suspect it's the environment

that's causing the overload, move to safer ground. Find a calming place to de-escalate the situation.

3. **Give praise.** Once the crisis begins to subside, give your child some positive verbal feedback as he or she starts to calm down. This will take him further into a calm state.

There are physical tools you can purchase to help your child stay calm if they're prone to tantrums caused by sensory overload.

- **Therapeutic blankets** that are weighted provide awareness of the physical body.
- **Pop-up tents** provide alone time and private space. You can supply the tent with some of your child's favorite things like books, toys, or stuffed animals.
- **Noise-cancelling headphones** are a wonderful idea to prevent sensory overload, particularly in public places like malls or playgrounds or even at home when there's a lot going on.

So what's the difference between a tantrum and a sensory meltdown?

A **tantrum** can occur when a child feels overwhelmed by people, noise, and various other inputs in general, but there's not one particular thing that might set him off. It's just an overload of everything at once.

A **sensory meltdown** involves at least one of the senses and is triggered by one particular thing. Your child may react to a bright light or particular type of light (sight), a particular noise that irritates him or her (sound), the taste of certain foods, smells of foods or candles, for example, or the feel of certain fabrics like a blanket or jacket (touch). Even temperature can have an effect.

1. Remove the child immediately from the cause of the meltdown to a safe location and help him or her calm down.
2. Don't grab or pull the child away. Always tell them where they're going—what you're doing.
3. If the child ordinarily speaks, he or she may not be able to at that moment. When the child calms down, try to find out what bothered him. If the child doesn't speak, think about things in the room he was in: a loud ticking clock, harsh voices, a baby crying, a flashing light or billboard, even a man with a hat and mustache can be frightening to a child.
4. If your child covers his face or ears, it may be the beginning sign that a meltdown is about to occur.

CAN YOU PREVENT FUTURE MELTDOWNS?

Do your homework. It's possible to prevent tantrums and meltdowns by looking for patterns and triggers. You can try to figure out what was going on immediately before the episode. What factors may have contributed to it? Make a list of anything you can remember that was going on and see if you spot a pattern.

Watch what he or she eats. Many foods can trigger reactions in children, such as sugar, gluten, and casein. Sugar and refined carbohydrates in particular can increase anxiety in adults and children due to blood sugar spikes.

Have a game plan. You must have an exit strategy to remove your child from the stressful situation when he or she becomes overwhelmed. Make sure you always have a favorite toy or special blanket that your child find's comforting.

No Pretend Play

"The young child cannot distinguish well between the real and the imaginary, between things that are possible and things that are merely made up". (Maria Montessori)

Stacy is the single mom who loves to bake and has successfully engaged her son, twenty-two-year-old Justin, in helping her with her baking projects. Keep in mind that although Justin is now a young adult, he suffers from learning disabilities. Stacy was stressing about her son's future and managed to turn it around by focusing on his strengths—good motor skills and a grand imagination.

"Before I realized how good Justin was at baking, well at least at mixing and designing, I was jealous of my sister's boy who was graduating from college. Let me say that I was not proud of this—of being jealous. There was no one to blame, especially not these two boys, Justin and my nephew.

"When Justin was a kid, one of the things I noticed about him was that he was not into playing with blocks or toys or things like that. He loved going to the park and watching the birds. He liked to look for snails near the stream and could spend quite a while watching a worm make its way into the soil in our yard.

"But on the days when the weather prohibited us from going outside, he would spend time watching me bake. He really didn't seem to want to take part, but he would just sit there on a stool and quietly watch me, like he was simply fascinated or like he was some scientific observer. He had plenty of toys, but this interested him more.

"When he was about seven, my sister Anne came over for coffee and cake on a Sunday. This was something we did maybe twice a month. We sat at the kitchen table which was laid out with coffee mugs, cake plates, and a lemon cake I'd made that morning. It had a simple powdered sugar icing and I had placed a few very thin lemon slices curled in the center to make a sort of flower.

"When I went for the coffee pot, Justin began to take the mugs off the table. I'd used my big blue and white mugs which had cute sayings on them. I asked him why he was doing that. He didn't answer and Anne and I just looked at each other, puzzled. Justin proceeded to get a chair so he could reach the cabinet where the mugs were and brought down three yellow and white daisy-patterned mugs. He put them on the table exactly where I'd placed the blue mugs.

"We just started laughing. I said, 'Why didn't I think of that?' His powers of creative observation are amazing. Anne remarked he may be better than I am at this.

"It was actually my sister who gave me the idea to start a small home business and have Justin help me, and it's worked out beautifully."

Children believe what they see and generally can't tell the difference between reality and fantasy, usually up to the age of six when they begin to conceptualize. Children are great imitators who love to do whatever it is the adults are doing. They build creativity and imagination by doing things hands-on rather than just pretending to do them. For Justin, he'd observed his mother baking for several years before he actually took part in doing simple things. By the time he was into his late teens, he was fairly proficient at it.

In the beginning, Justin was 'mixing the ingredients' as a sort of play based on his observations of his mother. This is what he knew. He didn't actually know how to bake a cake other than the mixing, but his actions were recreating a scenario from his everyday experience.

"Once he did the coffee mug thing, I started thinking about his powers of observation. At the time, I didn't make the connection to his imagination or to creativity specifically. I would put Lincoln Logs in front of him and ask him to build a house or a fence or anything he wanted to build, but he wasn't interested at first. When I left the room for a moment and came back, he had arranged the logs into shapes: stars, flowers, even groups of flowers, not just a single flower. Now my own imagination caught fire. I went to Hobby Lobby and bought a few bags of colored glass stones and gave them to him. He came up with so many patterns that I was flabbergasted.

"Then I tried crayons, colored pencils and art supplies, but it didn't work. He didn't seem to get the idea that he could draw and color things until I hit on finger paints. Now he was really rolling. He could choose colors and 'draw' whatever he wanted. I showed him how to dip objects into paint, things from nature like leaves and pinecones and other things. And even though the paint was a bit messy, his designs weren't. They were relatively precise in their placement and his composition was wonderful. I'm going to try working with clay to see if he'll be able to make his own three-dimensional shapes. This is big in baking. He's been watching me make fondant into rosettes and so on, so we'll see."

When the concept was presented in a clear and precise form, and with her initial guidance, Justin was able to understand what Stacy wanted him to do. She kept it simple and real. She worked with a form of edible clay dough so he could actually eat his creations.

It's not unusual for individuals with autism to excel in one area. As he got older and his fine motor skills improved, he was able to distinguish how to make small petals and put them together. Right now, Stacy arranges them on the cakes she's creating for customers, but together they also make projects where Justin can go wild, doing whatever he wants in terms of decorating, or where he can make his own fondant shapes and arrange them as part of his training. Stacy is giving him ample opportunity to explore and experiment.

As Stacy puts it, "I have a lot of patience. Sometimes he'll get the decorations arranged and decide he doesn't like it, so he'll very carefully remove them and start all over. It can be a bit frustrating for me, but the end result is well worth it more times than not."

Attachment to Hard Inanimate Objects

> *"I believe that in approaching our subject with the sensibilities of statisticians and dissectionists, we distance ourselves increasingly from the marvelous and spell-binding imagination whose gravity drew us to our studies in the first place."* (Alan Moore, *Watchmen*)

Mike's child was fascinated by things that made no sense to Mike. His son David was four years old and didn't seem to want to play at anything—not cars or trucks or anything little boys usually play with. When he was finally evaluated and diagnosed with autism, Mike and his wife Jean were shocked.

"He was young enough where I wasn't embarrassed by any of his behavior, but other parents did sort of question it. He pretty much just stares at things, particularly things that don't move, like a chandelier or a painting. He looks like he's thinking, but when he gets into these trance-like states, he doesn't really respond to anything else around him. I just don't understand the fascination."

Colleagues at the Marcus Autism Center in Atlanta, Georgia, Children's Healthcare of Atlanta, and Emory University School of Medicine conducted an eye-tracking study of 109 autistic children and twenty-six non-autistic children using a video to track eye movements. What they observed was that these children were "more likely to notice the inanimate objects on the screen and less likely to watch the faces of those on the screen. Patterns [emerged] involving the degree and type of ASD. For example, highly verbal children tended to view people's mouths more often than the other children." (Rice, et al, 2012)

Anecdotal research suggest synesthesia may play a role in the fixation of inanimate objects amongst individuals with autism. Synesthesia is a condition where one sensory pathway automatically stimulates another sensory pathway. Basically, individuals experience a mixing of their senses, such as when you look at a fan and you taste chocolate.

Of the little we do know about synesthesia, there appears to be a strong and involuntary connection between the stimuli—in this case the inanimate object—and the sense that it triggers. This is referred to as associative synesthesia. But there's another type, projective synesthesia, where children see colors, forms, or shapes in response to a stimulus. So while an associative may react to the sound of a bell by seeing the color blue, for example, a projective might hear the bell and say it sounds like blue.

Consider the autistic child who can line up 100 Matchbox cars by color and style and know exactly which one was moved and by how much with precision accuracy. These autistic savants have learning disabilities but are extremely gifted in one area. Most often this area is related to memory: rapid calculation, music, even map-making. It's estimated that one in ten to one in two hundred autistics have savant syndrome to some degree. (Treffert, 2001)

The bottom line is this: we just don't know enough about the human mind to understand why these children are so fascinated or obsessed with inanimate objects.

> *"Fascination is much more enjoyable than frustration, and it's far more productive. By attempting to sincerely understand something, we become open and curious, which is a great starting point for learning and growth."* (Joseph Deitch, *Elevate: An Essential Guide to Life*)

Author's Note

"You can be the most beautiful person in the world and everybody sees light and rainbows when they look at you, but if you yourself don't know it, all of that doesn't matter. Every second you spend on doubting your worth, every moment that you use to criticize yourself; is a second of your life wasted."
(C. JoyBell C.)

I hope this book helps you process at least some of what you've been feeling so you're able to develop positive coping mechanisms that will help you deal with the stresses you will inevitably go through.

When raising children with ASD, parental stress becomes similar to military PTSD. The amount of stress parents go through is off the charts. Many develop high blood pressure, insomnia, obesity, anxiety, depression, and chronic fatigue as a result. Some secretly become alcoholics or drug users or have extramarital affairs to relieve the everyday tension and worry.

Some parents will find old emotions from their own childhood coming up. Individuals need to recognize displaced feelings from past experiences and check their own emotions against how they're applying their parenting techniques. Because of this, I also encourage visualization and positive energy development. Kids can sense when people are stressed.

I want to add value to the information parents, caretakers, and their families already have. In my practice, I offer advice that involves support groups, journaling, mediation, exercise, medication (for severe cases), hiring respite providers, making time for leisure activity (shopping, hair/nails, massages, girls or guys night out), prayer, therapy, acupuncture, yoga, and more.

Humor helps. You may think it's difficult to find humor in your situation, but consider the case of Denise who found joy in her daughter's pink-frosting hair. Find any bit of laughter you can and cherish those moments.

You may not have been aware that all of the feelings and emotions you're going through are common among parents of ASD children, and as a result, you've felt isolated and alone.

You don't need to suffer in silence. You don't need to neglect yourself or discount your feelings. You can take care of your sanity and still be devoted to your child. In fact, taking care of yourself will help you give better care, just like putting on your own lifejacket first.

If you haven't spoken to family members about how you're feeling, do so. They may or may not understand, but it will help to get it out of your system. You're bound to find a sympathetic ally. Join a support group if necessary.

Autism parenting magazines and blogs may provide insight into concerns, but my hope is that this book of journals, which highlights the emotional roller-coaster of raising a child with ASD, will give you a sense of belonging—a validation that can only come from others who have been there.

ASD kids are very sensible. They recognize energies. They are very intuitive and feed off the energy of others. Sometimes parents think they are calming the child down but instead they escalate the problem with constant nagging and/or shadowing.

I learned to use a very soft voice when my son had tantrums. I wanted him to learn how to express himself without having a meltdown. He is very calm now and independent but I had to learn the hard way.

During my era, we didn't have as many resources. It wasn't like it is today, where autism is beginning to go mainstream. So I learned to adjust to his learning style while introducing him to my world. I learned to embrace his world and he is welcoming my world. It's the perfect synergy

Practice self-care. Do something you enjoy. If you need to, call in a respite worker so you have a few hours to yourself. Even just going for a walk will ground you with nature, which has an immense healing and centering effect on humans. If you have a spouse who can take care of your child for the day, go out and enjoy a spa day. For married couples who want to spend a few hours alone together, a trusted relative or respite worker will be helpful. Do what makes you happy and you'll return better equipped to handle your obligations to your family.

Do something new or different. Even on the best of days, we all end up doing the same things over and over again. Routines are necessary and seldom change. If you can find something you've never done and the time to do it, you'll give yourself a shot of rejuvenation that can only come from exploring something new.

There was a time when autism was considered to be a type of mental illness. And like all "mental illnesses", we've learned that these conditions can be controlled, conditioned, and trained to a degree using coping mechanisms so sufferers can lead a relatively normal life.

There was also a time when some doctors were recognizing what they referred to as "sensitives"; people who felt more and who were able to "see through" others. These people generally did not get on well with crowds, loud noises, and could not see value in frivolous "partying". Their families may have said they're 'too sensitive for their own good'. Most of these people would be adults today and would appear to be somewhat unsociable, but we now know this is a form of social anxiety, something that may fit into the Spectrum.

The human brain and mind are the current frontier—a frontier about which scientists know relatively little. Tomorrow we'll know more just as today we know more than we knew fifty or ninety years ago.

There are a lot of 'what ifs' to be explored. Autistic people are highly aware of their environments. Learning to adapt and finding where you and your child fit into the world in your own ways is your challenge. Don't overanalyze. Learn and be in the moment and eventually you'll find that you do fit in, just in a different way—your own way.

Where Are They Now?

You may be curious to know how some of the people in this book have fared since the first writing. Each of them have gotten to know their children better and have found ways to cope—some of them ingenious. Not only have they helped their children, but they've managed to make their own lives better in the process.

These are Their Stories

Sandy, our energetic healthy nurse, was shocked when she received her child's diagnosis.

"I did go through all the classic stages of grief, and as a nurse, I was able to recognize that. It was like I was standing outside myself and watching one of my patients. It was that clear to me. I knew I had to go through it, but in the back of my mind was my new reality.

"Once I got past the initial shock of this whole thing, I realized I had to take some kind of action. I've always been a healthy eater because I know food plays a great part in health, so I reasoned that there was something I could do with that for James. I started doing my research and homework.

"The initial damage was done and I was determined to undo at least part of it. If I couldn't do that with food, I'd find ways to get around this, to make James's life work. I wasn't about to just accept it.

"I completely changed his diet. And after finding out about the gut biome connection, I tweaked my own a bit, too. James is six now, and he does exhibit some slow learning, but I believe it might have been worse had I not made some course corrections."

Try clearing your child's gut from harmful pathogens. You may see an improvement in focus, temperament, and digestive issues. (See *The Nutrition Connection* in *Part Three*)

Jennifer, the overweight loner, remembers how angry she was when she was asked to remove her son, Marcus, from an expensive daycare center.

"Looking back, I guess it wasn't the end of the world, but at the time, I felt so helpless. I wanted to punch someone. But they were probably right. When I look at him now, and how much calmer he is, I can really see the possibilities. I can hardly believe how much a bad gut can affect behavior. Why don't pediatricians tell us this?"

More and more pediatricians are slowly beginning to recognize the value of the gut-brain connection. Most are not particularly ready to recommend a specific diet change, but anecdotal evidence is mounting.

Denise felt extremely guilty over the role she felt she might have played in her son's health because of her poor eating habits.

"I've always been a terrible eater and lazy about cooking, but now, after this, I've had a rude awakening. I was overweight, tired all the time, and had no interest in anything but sitting in front of the TV, eating of course.

"When I heard about the nutrition protocol that involved clearing the gut, my interest was sparked. As lazy as I was about cooking and eating, I knew this was something I had to do. I wanted to do it for Evan.

"On the upside, I've actually lost forty pounds and have a lot more energy. It's like I can think clearly now and actually have an active interest in taking part in life. As for Evan, he seems to be doing better. He's entering the third grade and is on a strict diet. He's not at the top of his class, but he's doing well and I'm proud of him. He's a good kid."

Evan had a large toxic overload because he was eating the same foods as Denise and was also subjected to them in the womb. On top of that, he was exposed to many environmental toxins because he was always in front of the TV with her and she used a lot of sprays to give her home a quick cursory cleaning. The air was toxic and filled with mold, dust mites, and chemicals. To her credit, she's come a long way in changing all that.

Matt is the now eight-year-old son of Morgan. He's the boy who jumped out of his father's Land Rover on their way to the mall.

"If it hadn't been so potentially dangerous, I'd think it was funny. How in the world did this kid manage to run half a mile to the candy store in just a few minutes? He hasn't stopped liking being in a candy store, or any store where there are a lot of colors. He seems most drawn to things like jelly beans, balloons, balls; things that are colorful and can be displayed in mounds, piles, or bunches.

"After that frightening day, I've made it a point, first of all, to never forget to engage the child safety locks. But we also go to the candy store quite regularly. We don't buy anything most of the time. Sometimes I'll buy something just so they let us keep coming back. I've actually explained to the owner about Matt's condition and he's been very understanding about it. What a blessing that's been.

"I don't know if he's simply outgrowing something or if these regular visits to the candy store are satisfying his curiosity, but he doesn't try to jump out of the car anymore, even when we pass a new place that might be of interest to him. Now he just points and yells 'store', and that's okay with me."

Curiosity among children is common, and may turn into obsession in autistic children. Morgan's idea of satisfying Matt's curiosity with regular visits to the candy store was a good one that worked for him. In this case, Matt didn't want the candy, which would have been detrimental to his health. He only wanted to look at the colors.

Tina's family was unsupportive of her daughter Emily's behavior at the family reunion, and Tina found herself embarrassed by it.

"My family hasn't changed much since that incident at the reunion. I guess they're just snobs [laughs]. But they are my family and it does hurt that they can't accept Emily. I mean, these are intelligent people with their heads stuck up their you-know-what. Autism is a big deal. I wonder how they'd behave if she had some other disease like cancer.

"Well I've made it a point to reject all their invitations. I'd rather have my daughter the way she is than them the way they are. It's a shame it had to turn out this way. Em seems to be doing well, though. Every now and then, she'll do something weird, or shall I say age inappropriate, but overall, she's okay. I just do my best to tell her calmly that that behavior is not acceptable and she doesn't repeat it. So she does understand."

Tina managed to handle the situation at the family reunion well and without making her daughter look or feel bad, and she continues to calmly relay proper behavior and social etiquette to Emily, who responds well to this.

Jeff, whose son Jacob stuffed Jeff's friend's toilet with paper, has made great strides in Jake's behavior.

"I was kind of at my wit's end with Jake. I joined a support group where I'd go once a week to sit around with other guys in my situation. I don't know if this is easier for women, but it's just not easy. Respite services came in and gave me two hours to myself, so at least there was that. I couldn't leave Jake home with Josh. Josh is a smart kid, but not able to handle this on his own, I was sure of that. I wouldn't do that to him.

"One of the guys there told me about this diet that took care of his kid. It had something to do with a wild proliferation of worms and fungi and all sorts of bacteria that were affecting his kid's brain. I didn't understand it at first, but I did look into it and began to try it on Jake.

It's been about two years now and he's calmed down so much. If I hadn't experienced it for myself, I wouldn't believe it. He doesn't run around the house looking to get into trouble and doesn't try to run after every little bird or butterfly outside. I think I did the right thing. He's like a different kid."

Jake's former behavior is classic. In this case, there was a dramatic difference, so noticeable that Jake seemed "like a different kid". You can believe in the power of real food as a healing agent and junk and chemicals as destroyers of the human body.

You'll remember John, Command Sergeant Major in the U.S. Army, now retired.

"When I got home [referring to his last tour of duty] it was like I didn't know my own son. Who was this kid? And why did he do the things he did? What made him tick? Those were all big questions and I wanted answers.

"I never did find out why he came out the way he did, but the months and days I've been spending with him have paid off. He's still obsessed with his cars and gets passing grades in school, but all the little things I learned in the service that I applied to his training have helped. He's much more responsive, and his teachers say the same thing.

"We take things one step at a time, one day at a time. I've learned to read him a little better, and this helps me understand and plan strategies to help us both. We've both grown. We still have a little crisis now and then, but it doesn't affect me as much as it did that first time because, as I said, I'm learning to understand."

John also made an effort to see that JJ's diet was on target. He spoke with the school and informed them of his restrictions when it came to food. John believes this is part of the reason the frequency of meltdowns has diminished. JJ's lessened sense of urgency and frustration when something is out of place has also greatly diminished.

Shannon, the lawyer turned homemaker, was resentful of her husband's freedom to come and go while she was tied to the house and kids.

"I really can hardly believe I let things get that bad. I almost allowed my marriage to fail because I wasn't taking care of my needs and I wasn't being honest with my husband about them and how I was feeling.

"We're over that hump though. Now I make it a point of getting a pedicure and manicure as part of my monthly routine. I go to the gym every other day and on the alternate days, I exercise at home. Respite care has helped me greatly in that regard. They allowed me the time to take care of myself.

"Mike has arranged to spend at least one workday a week at home and has made it a point to spend at least one day on the weekend with the family. His support has helped keep our marriage together and the kids love having him around. Occasionally he'll get caught up in work at home but it's not too often, so that's okay. He'll catch himself, and I know he wouldn't be doing it if it were not important."

Shannon found the courage to be honest to herself and her husband about her needs. As soon as that was resolved, all her resentment vanished. Search yourself if you're feeling this way, even if you're single. Your resentment will manifest itself in all aspects of your life. Take care of yourself. You don't need to be a martyr. There are resources to help you.

Sweet Denise with the pink hair was deeply saddened by the fact that almost no one showed up for her daughter's birthday party.

"People can be cruel. I already knew that, but I never felt it so deeply. I mean, my own family? They couldn't put up with it for a few hours? In a way I'm kind of glad it all turned out the way it did. I may never have seen Melanie's heart the way I did when she handed me that cupcake. And the pink icing hair! What a scream! I love that kid.

"My mom called me the next morning and asked if she could come over. She had something she wanted to discuss with me. I had no idea what it was, but I was a bit apprehensive. I had a feeling it was going to be a 'kind' lecture about Melanie, or something equally self-righteous.

"As it turned out, Mom had a handout about a new theory, something called the gut-brain connection. It was quite detailed. Mom was not intrusive or pushy about it. She just told me it was worth looking into.

"It all made sense. And here I was making cupcakes with sugary pink icing. Just the thing this handout was telling me was the wrong thing to do. In fact it went so far as to say it could be contributing to Melanie's behavior.

"Well, I like to cook, so I took it to heart immediately and within three weeks I began to see Melanie calming down all around. It was like a miracle. No exaggeration."

The gut-brain connection is more than just a theory. There's solid research regarding the neurological connection between the gut and brain. But when people think of the gut, most of them think only of the stomach. In reality, the gut or gastrointestinal tract comprises everything from the mouth to the intestines at the other end and everything in between where food passes through.

Interestingly, many neurotransmitters are produced by the microbes living there, some of which control feelings of depression, social and general anxiety, stress, and fear.

Angela and Don have an adult daughter, Marilyn, who has a fondness for eating soap, and they worry constantly about her future well-being.

"Marilyn is still working, thank God. I don't think we need to worry about her in that respect. She gets around well. But we had a big scare when she started that soap-eating thing.

"I learned that it had to do with a mineral deficiency, which we've since cleared up. Part of the problem was that she wasn't absorbing minerals for some reason. We sought a naturopathic doctor and she suggested beginning with organic and pastured foods only. This, according to her, would begin reducing any toxic overload.

"We went through quite a long process with cleaning up her diet, and we ate the same foods we prepared for her. It took about six months before we started to see an improvement, but now she checks out okay in the mineral department. And she's stopped craving soap. I feel so relieved. Sometimes we just don't realize how something so potentially life-threatening can be healed by something as simple and available as the right food."

Many soaps contain salt and other minerals, particularly if you're using a soap that has the word 'mineral' in its name, such as Dead Sea Minerals, or Dial's new Sea Minerals Enriching Body Wash, to name just two. But the minerals are not the problem, it's the other ingredients that are potentially deadly. Soaps contain chemical anti-bacterial agents, lye (caustic soda), talc, and numerous other harmful chemical ingredients. (See *The Toxic Exposure Connection* section of this book, *What's in Commercial Products?*)

Casey has two children on the Spectrum, one with Asperger's and the other with PDD.

"Brad is nine now and is doing fine. He's manageable, but Britt still has some mood swings, although she's a lot better than she was two years ago. Oh, my God! She was literally out of control—biting, hitting, and tantrums every single day.

"When I was told about how the body harbors toxins and viruses and mold and all kinds of other things that are harmful—that can affect the brain through the intestines—I started thinking it would be worth a try. I didn't want to be like this anymore and I certainly didn't want my daughter to have to live her entire life like this. She was missing out on so much.

"Today, two years later, she's calmed down to the point where there are literally no more tantrums. She doesn't bite or lash out either. Maybe it's because of the behavioral training she's been getting or she's a little older now, but I think it has a lot to do with the new diet."

There are hundreds of examples of children who have been cleared of toxic overload and who have experienced life-changing differences in mood and behavior.

Stacy's story of opening a business as a result of wanting to give her son a future is outstanding.

"Justin is twenty-five now and business is booming. But here's something I found to be particularly eye-opening. When I first hit on the idea of starting a baking business and making Justin my partner, we were happy as clams, both of us tasting samples of our work and Justin licking the batter and frosting bowl the way little kids do. I didn't see anything wrong with that.

"But after a few months, when the initial fun had worn off, I realized it might not be such a great idea for either of us to be eating all that sugar. It was basically just on general principle. After all, there's enough information out there about the dangers of too much sugar.

"Within about three weeks, I noticed my own energy level go up. And more to the point, I noticed Justin's attention and alertness change. It seemed as though he was more connected to what we were doing. I didn't attribute it to the sugar at first, but then, as we both continued to improve, I managed to put two and two together.

"Now I'm working on creating recipes that are sugar free and I've managed to come up with a few flavors that include veggies. They're really tasty and are going over well with customers. Everyone wants to be healthy."

So here we have another example of how a simple change in diet made a difference in an autistic person's ability to learn.

Tonya is the mother of the twin boys, one with autism who was specifically left out of a party invitation.

"We've all been on the nutrition protocol for about a year now and Matt has improved significantly. I still feel a little bitter about the party thing. Even though he's a lot better now, why should I be friends with people who left me and my son out in the cold? I know I need to get over this for the boys' sake, but it's hard. I still feel lonely. I have my husband and we do a lot together, but why are people so mean?

Tonya would benefit from group counseling, if only to get past her resentment and feelings of loneliness and isolation. She would also benefit from socializing more with those outside her family. She and her husband could go out with other couples or to a club, just to be around others. They need a sense of perspective.

For Martin, there is nothing like a lot of love to heal the betrayal and harm that was done to him.

"I don't think I'll ever get over what they did to my boy. We did report it to the welfare board, and they said they would look into it. They also said this is not uncommon. It's been months and we haven't heard anything. I doubt we ever will. I'm just happy to have Martin home again."

The fact is that children with intellectual disabilities are greater than three times more likely to fall victim to abuse, particularly sexual abuse. For adult abuse, that number is about half.

The United Nations Convention on the Rights of Persons with Disabilities reinforces the need to protect the rights of children and adults with disabilities and ensure their full and equal participation in society. This includes avoiding the adverse experiences resulting from violence which are known to have a wide range of detrimental consequences for health and well-being. When prevention fails, care and support for children and adults who are victims of violence are vital to their recovery. The WHO/World Bank World report on disability outlines what works in improving health and social participation of people with disabilities and promotes deinstitutionalization. (Hughs, et al, 2012)

Sonia was exhausted from dealing with four boys. Her nine-year-old, Garret, is autistic.

"I knew I couldn't go on like that. Everything was suffering, including my marriage. It was bad enough my husband worked nights, but during the day, it was chaos, even after the kids were in school. I was smoking like a fiend and living on chips and pizza. And I looked a wreck. I knew there had to be a better way, and I finally found it.

"We've been on the nutrition protocol for six months. Everyone eats better. I really don't like cooking, so I do a once a week thing where I cook all day and freeze stuff for the week. Garrett has to be on a special diet so that takes more effort, but I can't believe the change in him. Not to mention the fact that I'm cutting down on smoking and have more energy. I can at least deal with everything better now. I'm not stressed all the time like I was before and the kids seem happier because of it, too."

It's takes a long time for chronic exhaustion to hit, and it comes from the unrelenting stress that occurs on a daily basis. When someone gets to that point, there's a danger of illness and disease manifesting because stress compromises the immune system.

Taking care of yourself is of the utmost importance. A little stress or the occasional exhausting day won't do you much harm, but see to your own needs. Find ways. Employ the use of respite services, talk to a trusted friend or family member, or join a support group.

The excitement Patricia felt when her ten-year-old daughter spoke her first words was overwhelming.

"I don't think I'll ever forget that day. A miracle truly did happen. She still doesn't say much or speak very often, but at least now she's using two-word and three-word phrases, plus the rare longer phrase. She still says 'want ice cream'. I've learned to make my own at home so it's extra delicious and personally satisfying. To be honest, it's really frozen yogurt sweetened with fruit, not sugar, but she doesn't know that and she likes it just the same. We celebrate once a week in honor of that day."

Patricia did take the time to use play therapy and spent many hours a week with her daughter doing this. She's made considerable progress considering Meghan was completely non-verbal up to the age of ten.

Inspiration

I know you love your child, imperfections and all. It is my hope that these additional words—the words of others—will inspire you to greatness; that they may give you inspiration to create a future for your children that brings them into a world of understanding, and to let you know that your pain and experience is shared by others.

Hope and love—nurture these in your life and cry no more. There is no sadness that can change the world for the better. Exhaust yourself with a final flood of tears, then let it all go and move towards a life of profound experiences, with each day bringing new possibilities along with the work and dedication you're putting in.

Together, with the minds of many like-thinking people, we can make the world a more forgiving and accepting place, not only for our autistic children, but for anyone who is outcast for some misunderstood condition, for hope and love are the better parts of the human spirit.

Carry a torch of courage and inspire others. Let laughter flow and find peace in your soul. De-idealize expectations and honor both your and your child's rhythm. Recognize your crisis, but know that you are not responsible for it. Enjoy your seconds of bliss and embrace the human angels who enter your life. Become a conduit for grace and never lose your flame.

I hope all of these things for you.

I'm an Autism Mom.
I cry when no one is looking.
I feel lonely with people there.
I hear the comments, feel the stares.
But no one seems to care.
I have to stay strong.
I can't give up.
I need to keep my head up.
This journey won't be easy.
I know it won't be.
But my child's needs.
Is what matters to me.
(www.theautismworld.com)

"*Nothing can dim the light which shines from within.*" (Maya Angelou)

"*Sometimes when you least expect it, the tables turn and that scary feeling that has taken hold of you for so long somehow turns into hope.*" (David Archuleta, *Chords of Strength: A Memoir of Soul, Song and the Power of Perseverance*)

"*There was no need for a term like 'magical thinking' in the Golden Age of Man... children were not mocked or scolded in those days for singing to the rain or talking to the wind.*" (Anthon St. Maarten, *Divine Living: The Essential Guide to Your True Destiny*)

"*Your child's magic will find you if you learn to listen with soul, not ear, to their quiet secrets, deep beyond all dreams.*" (Lee Caleca)

"My mind is on a more important thing that lifts my heart and makes my spirit soar. I want to make the souls of people sing and quiet down the mean and bullying roar. To help the wounded replace the scar with the right to be exactly who they are." (Nancy Rue)

"The laces, untied, the socks won't match. I won't know what to wear and when to wear it and I am rubbish at the small talk required to fit into places. There are square pegs that spend their lives trying to squeeze into round holes, but I wasn't even given four straight sides. I am shapes when none are required, I am a million wrongs stuffed into something. I never asked if it was right. I am this, and I've never been that, and I've no plans to remedy the broken bits." (Tyler Knott Gregson, *Wildly Into the Dark*)

"You can't expect everyone to have the same dedication as you." (Jeff Kinney, *Diary of a Wimpy Kid*)

"These are the few ways we can practice humility. To speak as little as possible of one's self. To mind one's own business. Not to want to manage other people's affairs. To avoid curiosity. To accept contradictions and correction cheerfully. To pass over the mistakes of others. To accept insults and injuries. To accept being slighted, forgotten and disliked. To be kind and gentle even under provocation. Never to stand on one's dignity. To choose always the hardest." (Mother Teresa)

"Take care not to listen to anyone who tells you what you can and can't be in life." (Meg Medina)

"Difference is an accident of birth and it should never be the source of hatred or conflict. Respect it. Respect is the fundamental principle of peace." (John Hume)

"The things that we share in our world are far more valuable than those that divide us." (Donald Williams)

"Remember to look up at the stars and not down at your feet. Try to make sense of what you see and wonder about what makes the universe exist. Be curious. And however difficult life may seem, there is always something you can do and succeed at. It matters that you don't just give up." (Stephen Hawking)

"The real voyage of discovery does not consist of seeking new landscapes, but in having new eyes." (Marcel Proust)

About the Author

Dr. Sharline Mashack, DNP is an experienced board-certified Psychiatric Mental Health Nurse Practitioner who specializes in treating various conditions, from ADHD to Schizophrenia. She uses a holistic approach to prescribe medications and provide psychotherapy and education to her patients and their families.

She began her studies after her son was diagnosed with autism, and as a military spouse, Dr. Mashack has worked in several areas of the healthcare system, gaining knowledge and experience from leaders in the field. She has now focused her career on using a holistic and integrative approach to empower families of children and adults with challenging emotional and behavioral issues, including autism and other mental health disorders.

The lack of social support and challenges that are typical for special needs parents led to an inherent desire to help thousands of parents of children with disabilities.

Revered by her patients as a compassionate and competent provider, Dr. Mashack is passionate about improving emotional well-being in the lives of special needs families to cope with worry, loneliness, guilt, and unknowing self-destruction.

Outside of work, she enjoys spending quality time with her husband and two sons, traveling to exotic places, exploring new adventures, and making others smile.

Discover the power to create a new reality at
www.drmashack.com.

References

American Psychiatric Association (APA). 2000. *Diagnostic and statistical manual of mental disorders: DSM-IV-TR*. Washington, DC: American Psychiatric Association.

Arora, M., Reichenberg, A., Willfors, C., Austin, C, Gennings, C., Berggren, S., Lichtenstein, P., Anckarsater, H., Tammimies, K., & Bolte, S. (2017). "Fetal and postnatal metal dysregulation in autism." Nature Commununications; doi: 10.1038/NCOMMS15493 [Online 1 June 2017]

"Autism Spectrum Disorder". (n.d.) National Institute of Mental Health (NIMH). U.S. Dept. of Health and Human Services. Accessed June 17, 2019. https://www.nimh.nih.gov/health/topics/autism-spectrum-disorders-asd/index.shtml

Bleuler, E. (1911). "Dementia Praecox or the Group of Schizophrenias". As cited in Moskowitz, A., Heim, G. (2011). *Schizophrenia Bulletin*, Volume 37, Issue 3, May 2011, pp 471-479. Oxford Academic https://academic.oup.com/schizophreniabulletin/article/37/3/471/1893651

"Blue light has a dark side. What is blue light? The effect blue light has on your sleep and more." (2012). *Harvard Health Letter*. Harvard Health Publishing, Harvard Medical School. Updated Aug 2018 https://www.health.harvard.edu/staying-healthy/blue-light-has-a-dark-side

Bowen, Richard. (n.d.) "The Enteric Nervous System." *Vivo Pathophysiology*. Colorado State University. Accessed June 30, 2019. http://www.vivo.colostate.edu/hbooks/pathphys/digestion/basics/gi_nervous.html

Calafat, A.M., Wong, L-Y., Ye, X., Reidy, J.A., & Needham, L.L. (2008). "Concentrations of the sunscreen agent benzophenone-3 in residents of the United States: National Health and Nutrition Examination Survey 2003–2004." *Environmental Health Perspectives.* July; 116(7):893-7. doi: 10.1289/ehp.11269

"Compliance Program Guidance Manual. Program 7329.001." (2007) Food and Drug Administration. *Chapter 29 – Colors and Cosmetics Technology.*
https://www.fda.gov/media/78441/download

"Environmental Working Group comments to Food and Drug Administration: a survey of ingredients in 25,000 personal care products reveals widespread use of nana-scale materials not assessed for safety in everyday products." (2010) Nano Ethics Bank. Illinois Institute of Technology. https://ethics.iit.edu/NanoEthicsBank/node/1538

Evans, Bonnie. (2013) "How autism became autism: The radical transformation of a central concept of child development in Britain." History of the Human Sciences. *SAGE*, Volume 26 Issue 3, pp3-31. doi: 10.1177/0952695113484320

"EWG Research Shows 22 Percent of All Cosmetics May Be Contaminated With Cancer-Causing Impurity." (2007) Environmental Working Group. https://www.ewg.org/news/news-releases/2007/02/08/ewg-research-shows-22-percent-all-cosmetics-may-be-contaminated-cancer

"Exposures Add Up – Survey Results." (2004) Environmental Working Group (EWG). https://www.ewg.org/skindeep/2004/06/15/exposures-add-up-survey-results/

"FDA authority Over Cosmetics: How Cosmetics are not FDA Approved, but are FDA Regulated." (2018) U.S. Food and Drug Administration. Accessed July 1, 2019
https://www.fda.gov/cosmetics/cosmetics-laws-regulations/fda-authority-over-cosmetics-how-cosmetics-are-not-fda-approved-are-fda-regulated

Foldy, Csabe, Malenka, Robert C., Sudhof, Thomas. (2013) "Autism-Associated Neuroligin-3 Mutations Commonly disrupt Tonic Endocannabinoid Signaling." *Neuron.* Volume 78, Issue 3, P498-509, May 2013. Doi.org/10.1016/j.neuron.2013.02.036

Gamakaranage, C. (2016) "Heavy Metals and Autism." *Journal of Heavy Metal Toxicity and Diseases.* 2016, 1:3. http://heavy-metal-toxicity-diseases.imedpub.com/heavy-metals-and-autism.php?aid=17209

Gomez, E., Pillon, A., Fenet, H., Rosain, D., Duchesne, M.J., & Nicolas, J.C., et al. (2005). "Estrogenic activity of cosmetic components in reporter cell lines: parabens, UV screens, and musks." *Journal of toxicology and environmental health* 68(4): 239-251 [PubMed] https://www.ncbi.nlm.nih.gov/pubmed/15799449

Gray, T.J., Gangolli, S.D. (1986). "Aspects of the testicular toxicity of phthalate esters." Environmental health perspectives [NCBI] March 25, 65: 229-23.
https://www.ncbi.nlm.nih.gov/pmc/articles/PMC1474678/

Hauser, R., Meeker, J.D., Singh, N.P., Silva, J.J., Ryan, L., Duty, S., & Calafat, A.M. (2007) "DNA damage in human sperm is related to urinary levels of phthalate monoester and oxidative metabolites." *Hum Reprod.* 2007;22(3):688-95. [PubMed]

Hosie, Suzanne, et al. (2019). "Gastrointestinal dysfunction in patients and mice expressing the autism-associated R451C mutation in neuroligin-3." Wiley Online Library. *Autism Res 2019.* © 2019 International Society for Autism Research, Wiley Periodicals, Inc. https://onlinelibrary.wiley.com/doi/full/10.1002/aur.2127

Hughes, K., Bellis, M.A., Jones, L., Wood, S., Bates, G., Eckley, L., McCoy, E., Mikton, C., Shakespeare, T., & Officer, A. (2012) "Prevalence and risk of violence against adults with disabilities: a systematic review and meta-analysis of observational studies." Dept. of Violence and Injury Prevention and Disability. World Health Organization. *Lancet* 2012; doi:10.1016/S0410-6736(11)61851-5. https://www.thelancet.com/journals/lancet/article/PIIS0140-6736(11)61851-5/fulltext

"Ingredients found unsafe for use in cosmetics (11 total, through February 2012)." (2012) Cosmetic Ingredient Review (CIR). http://www.cir-safety.org/sites/default/files/U-unsafe%202-02-2012%20final.pdf

Kang, Dae-Wook, et al. (2013) "Reduced Incidence of Prevotella and Other Fermenters in Intestinal Microflora of Autistic Children." PLOS ONE.

https://journals.plos.org/plosone/article?id=10.1371/journal.pone.0068322

Kasari, Connie, Tager-Flusberg, Helen, Cooper, Judith. (2010) NIH Workshop on Nonverbal School-Aged Children with Autism. National Institute on Deafness and Other Communication Disorders. U.S. Department of Health & Human Services: National Institutes of Health.
https://www.nidcd.nih.gov/research/workshops/nonverbal-school-aged-children-autism/2010/summary

Law, Paul MD, MPH, Anderson, Connie, Ph.D. (2011) "IAN RESEARCH REPORT: ELOPEMENT AND WANDERING." Interactive Autism Network. IAN Project, April 2011
https://www.iancommunity.org/cs/ian_research_reports/ian_research_report_elopement

Lord, C., Risi, S., DiLavore, P.S., Shulman, C., Thurm, A., & Pickles, A. (2006) "Autism from 2 to 9 years of age". Arch Gen Psychiatry. Jun; 63(6):694-701 [NCBI]
https://www.ncbi.nlm.nih.gov/pubmed/16754843?dopt=AbstractPlus

Miller, Judith Ph.D., Gabrielsen, Terisa P., Farley, Megan, Speer, Leslie, Villalobos, Michele, & Baker, & Courtney N. (2015) "Identifying Autism in a Brief Observation." *Pediatrics*. February 2015, Volume 135 Issue 2 https://pediatrics.aappublications.org/content/135/2/e330

Milman, O. (2007) "Lead in Lipstick." Campaign for Safe Cosmetics (CSC). Accessed July 1, 2019 http://www.safecosmetics.org/get-the-facts/regulations/us-laws/lead-in-lipstick/

Oelofsen, N., Richardson, P. (2006) "Sense of coherence and parenting stress in mothers and fathers of preschool children with developmental disability." *Journal of Intellect & Developmental Disability*. 2006 Mar; 31(1):1-12 https://www.ncbi.nlm.nih.gov/pubmed/16766317

Rice, Katherine Ph.D., Moriuchi, Jennifer M., Jones, Warren, & Klin, Ami. (2012) "Parsing Heterogeneity in Autism Spectrum Disorders: Visual Scanning of Dynamic Social Scenes in School-Aged Children." *Journal of the American Academy of Child and Adolescent Psychiatry*. 2012 Mar. Volume 51, Issue 3 [PubMed]
https://www.ncbi.nlm.nih.gov/pubmed/22365460

Rutter, Michael. (1972) "Childhood Schizophrenia Reconsidered", *Journal of Autism and Childhood Schizophrenia*. Volume 2, Issue 3, pp 315-337: 315–37
https://link.springer.com/article/10.1007%2FBF01537622

Schreurs, R.H., Legler, J., Artola-Garicano, E., Sinnige, T.L., Lanser, P.H., Seinen, W., et al. (2004). "In vitro and in vivo antiestrogenic effects of polycyclic musks in zebrafish." *Environmental Science & Technology*. Feb. 15; 38(4): 997-1002 [PubMed]
https://www.ncbi.nlm.nih.gov/pubmed/14998010

Treffert, Darold A. (2009) "The savant syndrome: an extraordinary condition. A synopsis: past, present, future." *Philosophical Transactions of the Royal Society of London. Series B, Biological Sciences*. May 27, 364(1522):1351–7 [NCBI]
https://www.ncbi.nlm.nih.gov/pmc/articles/PMC2677584/

"The Trouble with Ingredients in Suncreens: EWG's 2019 Guide to Suncreens." (2019) Environmental Working Group. Accessed July 01, 2019
https://www.ewg.org/sunscreen/report/the-trouble-with-sunscreen-chemicals/

Veldhoen, N., Skirrow, R.C., Osachoff, H., Wigmore, H., Clapson, D.J., Gunderson, M.P., et al. (2006). "The bactericidal agent triclosan modulates thyroid hormone-associated gene expression and disrupts postembryonic anuran development." *Aquatic Toxicology* (Amsterdam, Netherlands) Dec 1;80(3): 217-227 [PubMed]
https://www.ncbi.nlm.nih.gov/pubmed/17011055

Von Eschenback, Andrew C. M.D. (2007). "Cosmetics with banned and unsafe ingredients." Accessed June 21, 2019.
https://www.ewg.org/news/testimony-official-correspondence/cosmetics-banned-and-unsafe-ingredients

Wolff, M.S., Engel, S.M., Berkowitz, G.S., Ye, X., Silva, M.J., Zhu, C., Wetmur, J., & Calafat, A.M. (2008). "Prenatal phenol and phthalate exposures and birth outcomes." Environ Health Perspect. 2008 Aug; 116(8):1092-7 [PubMed]
https://www.ncbi.nlm.nih.gov/pubmed/18709157

Resources

100 Day Autism Parenting Kit:
https://www.myautism.org/wp-content/uploads/2015/01/100-Day-Kit.pdf

Back-to-School Preparation for Children with Autism:
https://www.myautism.org/back-school-preparation-children-autism/

College Programs for Students with Autism:
https://www.myautism.org/college-programs-students-autism/

Finding a Summer Camp:
https://www.myautism.org/tips-finding-summer-camp/

Genetic Testing for Autism:
https://www.myautism.org/wp-content/uploads/2016/01/Genetic-Testing-for-Autism.pdf

Housing Assistance for Families with Autism:
https://www.myautism.org/wp-content/uploads/2016/01/Housing-Assistance-for-Families-with-Autism.pdf

Integrated Classes for Students with High Functioning Autism:
https://www.myautism.org/wp-content/uploads/2016/01/Education-Information.pdf

Noise-Cancelling Headphones:
https://www.friendshipcircle.org/blog/2012/03/21/8-headphones-for-children-with-autism-and-auditory-processing-disorder/

Parent's Guide to Bullying:
https://www.myautism.org/wp-content/uploads/2015/01/Parents-Guide-to-Buillying.pdf

Pop-up Tents:
https://alleviateautism.com/effective-products/

Recreational Activities for Children on the Spectrum:
https://www.myautism.org/recreational-activities-children-spectrum/

2019 Guide to Sunscreens:
https://www.ewg.org/sunscreen/
https://draxe.com/best-sunscreens/

Therapeutic Blankets:
https://www.sensacalm.com/collections/custom-weighted-blankets

Therapies (General) for Individuals with Autism:
https://www.myautism.org/wp-content/uploads/2016/01/General-Therapies-for-Individuals-with-Special-Needs.pdf

Therapy Tools and Toys for Children with Autism:
https://www.myautism.org/toys-children-autism/
https://therapyshoppe.com/products/P4499-speech-therapy-products-recorders-educational-teaching-tools-fidgets-chewy-tubes
http://www.autismtoysandmore.com/

www.ingramcontent.com/pod-product-compliance
Lightning Source LLC
Chambersburg PA
CBHW051352070526
44584CB00025B/3738